London Borough of Hamm

FULHAM L
598 FULHAM RO
(736 11

Please return this book to the Library from which it was borrowed on or before the last date stamped. Fines will be charged on overdue books at the rate currently determined by the Borough Council.

DORSET co			
9/4/83 + 2			

Renewal may be made by post, telephone or personal call, quoting details immediately above and the last date stamped.

in
Memory
of
ALISTAIR AND ESTHER
A brother and sister beloved

ONE OF THE
RICHEST
GIFTS

An Introductory Study of the Arts
from a Christian World-view

JOHN WILSON

The Handsel Press
1981

Published by
The Handsel Press Ltd.
33 Montgomery Street, Edinburgh

Paperback ISBN 0 905312 17 1

First published 1981

© 1981 The Handsel Press Ltd.

Printed in Great Britain by
Clark Constable Ltd, Edinburgh

CONTENTS

v

INTRODUCTION

The arts are among the richest gifts of God to mankind. Painting, sculpture, music, literature, drama, poetry, indeed all the crafts of men, can enthral and thrill. They can cheer the heart, stimulate the mind and enrich human experience and emotions. Life would be infinitely impoverished if there were no arts to challenge and delight.

Yet this celebration of creativity, in being able to make new and wonderful things, leaves many Christians uncomfortable. Where do the arts fit into the Christian life? Christians are often uncertain in their approach, understanding and contribution to the arts. Some take refuge in the assertion that they are of the 'world' and should be avoided. Some see the arts as the handmaid of evangelism and would use their emotive power to manipulate 'souls' into the Kingdom of God. Others assume that all music is sacred, poetry is the language of heaven, and artists are the prophets of truth.

Rather than walk in these false paths a genuine Christian understanding is needed; a Christian, biblically-based alternative. An approach that recognises that the arts are a gift of God, that can see their glory — and their limitations: not a search for a cosy Christian art, but an art that is dynamic, relevant and true.

This book is an attempt to consider a positive Christian approach which is both faithful to the Gospel and the arts. It is an attempt to understand and to contribute. Firstly, it is necessary to define the subject and see that the arts are not given for an educated or social élite, they are for all to enjoy and appreciate and are much more than mere entertainment. Then, in the confusion of the contemporary scene, there is the need to listen to what is being said in the arts of today and, perhaps more important, to appreciate why it is being said in our generation.

Analysis is not enough; there must be a constructive Christian approach. There is a need to see that the Christian Gospel is concerned with all of life and carries, not only the message of individual salvation, but the principles necessary for the cultural and social wellbeing of mankind. Indeed to see afresh that the Word of God can be a light to the arts and a guide to the path they should take. Finally, there is the need to work out a positive Christian contribution to the arts of our day.

In my approach to the subject I make no apologies for frequently quoting John Calvin. Although he is generally considered to have had a 'pathological hatred' of art and beauty, when he is allowed to speak for himself the myth is destroyed. He valued the arts as a gift given 'for God's glory and our good' and saw that they had an important role to play in human life. Recognising that we have suffered from this myth in Scotland I have added an appendix, seeking to challenge the findings of unthinking mythology by raising questions and making some preliminary observations on the subject of 'Scotland, Calvin and the Arts'.

I am aware that this is only an introductory study to a complex and challenging area of our common life. It is written in the hope that it will stimulate discussion and perhaps encourage Christians, not only to enjoy the arts which God has given, but to contribute by using their gifts of imagination and craftsmanship to 'God's glory and our good.' Much prayer, study and work remains to be done before the healing of the Gospel can be brought to the bruised body of the arts and harmony restored to the confusions of our culture.

PART ONE

WHAT IS ART?

1

WHAT IS ART?

The arts have always been part of human life. Even before the dawn of recorded history men decorated earthen pots, cooking utensils, weapons of hunting and war, and have left traces of their artistic skill in caves, burial chambers and places of worship. Almost every primitive community appeared to have its own craftsmen, making not only tools and weapons, but objects for worship or personal adornment. Stories and poems from the dawn of history have been handed down and the ancient Greeks had a highly developed theatre. In the medieval world Mystery, Miracle and Morality Plays were performed first in the Church and then in the market place. Paintings and sculpture were brought into the churches as 'books for the illiterate'. The arts were for everyone.

So throughout the centuries, in every society and culture, artistic objects, ritual, story, poetry, song and dance have had an important place in communal life. Although often related to religious life the arts have always had a wider appeal, bringing pleasure in mundane tasks such as songs for work and stories for relaxation. People have always been in contact with the arts in some form or other.

Today there is the opportunity of enjoying artistic offerings in ways unknown to previous generations. The finest literature is freely available from public libraries and paperback books are still comparatively cheap. Music of all kinds is readily available on record or tape, and radio and television brings music, drama and poetry into the home. Today the arts are available to all.

But what is art? Augustine confessed that, although he knew what time was, he would not know how to reply if someone asked him, 'what is time?' His words could apply to art; we know what it is but how can we answer the question? Art, in the broad sense of the word, includes painting, sculpture, music, dance, literature, drama, poetry and architecture – but what makes it 'art'? What is the difference between a child's drawing of himself and a Rembrandt self-portrait? What basic difference is there between a nursery rhyme and a Wordsworth poem? Is there a distinct difference between a simple pop song and a Beethoven sonata? Is there a difference of kind rather than degree?

It is not difficult to see why the question, 'what is art?' has haunted the minds of men since first the Greek philosophers started to ask questions about life, society and the world. The question is further complicated in our age for two reasons. Firstly, because the word has changed its meaning over the centuries and, secondly, by the way much modern art has developed, almost defying definition.

Craft into Art

The word 'art' has changed its meaning over the years. Originally the word simply meant craft or skill and was applied to all physical and intellectual ability; practical skill in woodwork or stone, or intellectual ability in subjects such as logic or grammar, was considered an 'art'. The older universities still give an 'arts' degree for even such studies as science, economics or philosophy. So for centuries the artist was seen as a craftsman and what we call art was simply a craft.

The idea of artistic objects being made simply to be admired did not arise. The ancient Egyptians carved beautiful statues of men, birds and beasts, not for exhibition, but for burying with their dead for religious reasons. The Romans had busts in their homes not for decoration, but as part of the cult of ancestor worship. The artist was a craftsman to supply what was needed.

Even when works of art began to be appreciated for their own worth, the artist was still seen as a craftsman who was there to produce what was wanted. Some of the greatest works of art in the Renaissance were commissioned with a firm brief; the artist was given strict instructions as to the size of the painting, content and even colours. Sculpture, music, poetry and even plays were produced to order.

Leonardo da Vinci, among his many other achievements, is recognised as one of the greatest artists of all times. In a letter to the Duke of Milan, Leonardo offered his services and listed his credentials for a post on the Duke's staff. He numbered them and they included qualifications such as being a military engineer able to construct bridges, battering rams, mines, covered chariots, guns and catapults, as well as being an architect and water engineer. Almost as an afterthought, without numbering the item, Leonardo adds, "I can carry out sculpture in marble, bronze or clay, and also I can do in painting whatever may be done as well as any other be he who he may." (1)

The artist was a craftsman, selling his wares almost like a merchant, and working to suit the needs of his patron or customer. But slowly, over the years from the Renaissance, there was a change in the attitude towards artists and the arts. By the 18th century a clear distinction was being made between the 'practical' arts and the 'fine' or 'beautiful', arts. Art was no longer seen as a mere craft but something higher and more important. The Fine Arts, as we know them, were born.

The 18th century 'Enlightenment' was a period of intense philosophical and literary activity. Reason became the new god. As knowledge became more 'scientific' the very concept of a God who had to reveal Himself was considered to be against reason and unacceptable; to believe in such a God, or in miracles, was dismissed as unreasonable. Although many of the philosphers still used the concept of God it was no longer the God of the Bible, but the God of the philosophers, the unknown God of the Deists, or the 'Supreme Reason' of the intellectuals of the French revolution.

As knowledge became more rational and human reason supreme the arts retreated from the findings and theories of the philosphers and scientists. The arts became Romantic in their approach and search for truth. Romanticism was a widespread movement which, in general, emphasised emotion against reason, intuition against logic and saw imagination as being of more importance than intellect. It was a reaction, a protest against the scientific approach of the Enlightenment.

Because Romanticism laid such importance upon originality, intuition, emotion and personal vision, it did tend towards individualism. So the concept of the artist as a lonely genius, separate from society, began to gain wide acceptance. He was no longer considered a simple craftsman working for patron or community but seen as a romantic genius set apart for an almost prophetic mission and ministry. It is interesting, and significant, that a great number of the artists of the period lived up to the new image; they were themselves romantic figures even apart from their work.

Beethoven composed music he would never hear. Byron scandalised his contemporaries by his moral behaviour and by ending his life while going off to fight for the liberty of Greece. Shelley led a rebellious life and his tragic death by drowning was followed by the romantic burning of his body after the manner of the ancient Greeks. Keats had a passionate love of beauty, but had a youthful death. In Scotland there was Robert Burns with his poverty and love of freedom, whisky and women, and in the Lake District there was the lonely, spiritual grandeur of William Wordsworth. All these added up to the image of the artist as a man apart, not quite at home in this world, and not subject to the normal rules, laws and conventions of other, mere mortal men.

As the artist became more apart so the arts became more mystical in that they were removed from the ordinary objects and activities of daily living. Artists almost became prophets creating a new religion and language. There was an obsession with Nature – always spelled with a capital 'N'. Nature was no longer part of creation to be described and appreciated; it was invoked almost as a god. Poems and prayers were made to Nature which was seen as the source of life, the bringer of comfort, and the cure for all ills. Indeed for one group of poets it appeared that the proper study of mankind was no longer man – or God – but the Lake District!

While all the arts have moved on from the Romantic period we have inherited their definition of the arts as being on a much higher plane than mere craftsmanship and the artist as being someone unique and important. The reverent hush in the Art Gallery, the respectful silence in the Theatre, the elegant audience at the Concert and the cultivated snobbishness found in all the arts is part of the inheritence of the Enlightenment and of the Romantic period.

Today, almost without thought, it is taken for granted that the artist is greater than the craftsman and the arts far removed from all other human activity. The arts are superior, mystical and transcendant. The fine arts – Painting, Sculpture, Music, Dance, Literature, Drama, Poetry and Architecture – must always have capital letters and be appreciated with a proper servile attitude. They are for the cultured, the academic, and those sensitive souls of a correct social standing that can appreciate the 'finer things in life.'

Yet, for most of the history of mankind, the arts were simply part and parcel of life. They were the crafts employed in all the joys and tears of the human experience.

Art without Craft

The shift in emphasis makes it difficult to define the word 'Art.' Another problem lies in the development of modern art. Much contemporary art seems to lack any form of craftsmanship. Indeed it is an age when anything, and everything, can go under the name of Art.

Paint, casually thrown on to a canvas, can be presented as an artistic masterpiece, and an old boot, a bicycle wheel, and even a glass of water have been exhibited as art objects. An American sculptor, commissioned to supply a work simply phoned a stonemason giving the dimensions of the stone he wanted and arranged for it to be delivered to the buyer without ever having seen it. A composer wrote four bars of music for the piano, intending that this score should be repeated for twenty-four hours; at the other end of such musical compositions, another composer presented 4 minutes, 33 seconds of total silence as his contribution to a Music Festival. In literature a form of 'Do-It-Yourself' novel was issued in a box with the chapters individually clipped together; the reader was invited to shuffle the chapters into any order and then read the book; he could then reshuffle and reread the book.

Among his other activities, Andy Warhol has made an eight-hour film which consists of a single continuous shot of the Empire State Building in New York. A play by Samuel Becket has no characters or dialogue and has a running time of less than a minute; it is called *Breath*. Jackson Pollock, the American founder of 'action painting' took away the personal application of paint to canvas by letting paint drip onto a canvas from holes punctured in a tin. Other pictures he created by erecting a screen between himself and the canvas so that he could not see what he was painting.

All of these, with a vast number of such artefacts and happenings, have been presented as examples of modern art. Often these are the works of serious and intelligent men who are striving to convey the full horror of their vision and there are many reasons why art should be irrational in an irrational age.

But one thing is clear; whatever else has disappeared in much contemporary art, the idea of craftmanship has gone. There is simply no craftsmanship involved in much of what passes for modern art. Walking round a modern Art Gallery, or listening to computer-composed music or poetry deliberately written without rhyme, rhythm or reason will show this to be true.

As C. S. Lewis has put it: "Many modern novels, poems and pictures, which we are browbeaten into 'appreciating', are not good works because they are not *work* at all. They are mere puddles of sensitivity or reflection. When an artist is in the strict sense working, he of course takes into account existing tastes, interests and capacity of his audience. These, no less than the language, the marble, the paint, are part of his raw material; to be used, tamed, sublimated, not ignored or defied. Haughty indifference to them is not genius; it is laziness and incompetence. You have not learned your job – but a puddle is not a work, whatever rich wines or oils or medicines have gone into it." (2)

Art can never spring ready-made from the mind; it involves labour and effort. Whatever may be produced by chance, or computer, cannot be a work of craftsmanship; neither can it be, in the original meaning of the word, a work of art. Work is needed to make imaginative, creative thinking into a reality that can be communicated to others. It is this 'work' which is missing from so much contemporary art.

Much of the cultural confusion of our age comes from this loss of the artist as craftsman. Indeed it has devalued art. If anything, or everything, can be art then there is no such thing as art.

But perhaps art is too important to be left to the artists.

Towards a Definition

Art exists and artists are men and women with distinct gifts. They have sensitivity, imaginative insight, intuition and the ability to mould their vision into verbal or visible forms. They have, in a large measure, the gift of creativity, and are able to use colours, shapes, sounds or words to make something new and wonderful.

Art exists and it is influential. Poets, according to Shelley, are the unacknowledged legislators of the world, and it is a fact that books have changed cultures and the history of civilisation. Music can stir the heart and capture the soul of a nation, setting it off in a different direction to the beat of a different drummer. Drama can educate and inspire movements and ideologies while architecture is the concrete realisation of a society's values and dreams. Painting and sculpture can create new idols to worship and serve. The arts appear to be many things capable of being a good or bad influence on life and society.

So what is art? It is a gift and all gifts come from God. This includes the arts. As John Calvin wrote: "For the invention of the arts, and other things which serve the common use and convenience of life, is a gift of God by no means to be despised, and a faculty worthy of commendation." (3)

The arts are part of the rich bounty God has given to the world of men. The sphere of imagination, intuition and creativity is as much part of God's creation as the sun, moon and stars. They are given, like all gifts, for His glory and our good. But the gifts of God are not bestowed fully developed so that no effort is required of the recipient; the man gifted with knowledge and wisdom once had to learn the alphabet. So it is with the arts and crafts, and we have lost this truth through the Romantic view of the artist and arts.

Creation of art is not a suddenly attained ability. It comes through hard work, learning to work and shape different materials, sounds and words, cultivating the ability to use various tools, and even inventing new tools for specific tasks. It requires the ability to experiment in seeing what can be done, seeking the limit of one's ability and the limitations of the material used. The possibility of being an artist may be inborn but it is only as the artist exercises and develops that ability can he become a true artist.

Art is the highest form of craftsmanship.

To see the arts as the finest form of craftsmanship is neither to devalue the arts or the artist. It is to return to the tradition that the artist is a servant — just as all men were created to be servants of God and one another. It is to see the arts, not as a mystical or snobbish pursuit for the culturally privileged, but existing for the benefit and enjoyment of all. It is to recognise art as one of the richest gifts of God to mankind and to rejoice in the creativity He has given to men and women.

So art is craftsmanship. The craftsmanship that reveals and explores reality by visual, verbal and sound language. It enriches our lives with splendour and excitement; extending our experience by giving fresh sensations and emotions; widens our perceptions by opening up new ideas and visions and, not least of all, brings delight and joy to the human heart.

2

THE PURPOSE OF ART

The arts are among the richest gifts of God to mankind. Some of this richness is shown by the fact that they can fulfil many functions and serve many purposes in human life. They are neither an exclusive gift for a select few nor an insignificant aspect of experience. The arts are for all, and for all of life.

John Calvin wrote that the arts were a gift of God given 'for His glory and our good', (1) and it is not hard to see how the arts have been used to the glory of God. From the artistic splendour of the furnishings of the Tabernacle to majestic Cathedrals and Churches, the finest artwork and craftsmanship have been created to show something of the glory and majesty of God. Music, dance, literature, poetry and painting have all been vehicles of praise. Indeed the very act of creativity is an expression of the glory of God for the gift is His alone.

The arts are also for our good. This is their purpose and meaning; that the life we know now may be enriched, our minds stimulated and our hearts thrilled. We should rejoice in the arts, recognising that, in the final analysis, the purpose and meaning of a gift does not lie in itself but in the giver.

As H. R. Rookmaaker, Professor of Art History at the Free University of Amsterdam, said: "Art . . . has its own meaning that does not need to be explained, just as marriage does, or man himself, or the existence of a par-ticular bird or flower or mountain or sea or star. These all have meaning because God made them. Their meaning is that they have been created by God and are sustained by Him. So art has a meaning as art because God thought it good to give art and beauty to mankind." (2)

God thought it good that we should have the arts so we should value the gift. They should not be reduced to mere entertainment, though art can bring joy and pleasure. Neither should they be seen as mere decoration, butter on the dry bread of life, though they can embellish life and sprinkle the night with stars. The arts are for more than delight and pleasure.

They are a means of extending our experience of being human and mortal; a means of exploring creation and opening up the riches of the world in which we are placed, and they give us another language to understand aspects of the truth.

Extending Experience

It is one of the functions of the arts to reveal areas and aspects of life which are beyond our immediate experience. They can show us facets of reality which would be, in the normal course of events, beyond use. The arts extend our experience and even our emotions.

It is a fact, and perhaps a blessing, that no man can be subject to the total range of human experience. We cannot all know the full extent of tortured hopes, dreads, desires, lusts, loves, greeds and the many other complex and terrifying capabilities of the human soul. We cannot know all the fears and phobias that affect people. We cannot all know the alcoholic's craving for drink; the drug addict's dependence which blots out all other emotions; the gambler's mania, or even the love of a mother for a crippled child or the burden of a Prophet.

But through the medium of the arts these, and all of life, can be made real. By exposing ourselves to works of true art we can vicariously rejoice or suffer and have a better understanding of the range and possibilities of being human. This is true at even the simplest level.

Few can know the loneliness and hardship involved in being a castaway on a Desert Island; but a novel like *Robinson Crusoe* can make emotions and experience real to our minds. Most people now have no memory of the First World War but there is the poetry of Owen, Sassoon, Graves, and the many other poets who lived or died in the trenches or the mud of the battlefields. There are novels, paintings, plays, films and music showing in agonised depths the horror and glory, the brutality and humanity, displayed in the senseless abomination of such a war. Such art can reveal in a more intense and human fashion a truth that can never be disclosed in history books or tables of statistics.

Again, few in our country have had any experience of living in a totalitarian régime nor know anything of the trauma of a midnight arrest or the depersonalising monotony of State Labour Camps. But there are the novels and writings of artists such as Alexander Solzhenitsyn who can make us share, taste, smell and almost fully experience the dehumanisation of the individual in such a situation. Art can show the human condition in a way that cannot be achieved by any other medium.

The arts are powerful because they speak at the deepest level and deal with universals; the personal can be universally true, and the universal can be personalised. This is why Aristotle was able to argue that "poetry is something more philosophical and more worthy of serious attention than history; for while poetry is concerned with universal truths, history deals with particular facts." (3)

So the arts involve us in universal experiences and can shock us into an awareness that scale and remoteness often cancel. In an age of mass communications and instant news it is easy for sensitivity and pity to become callous. By probing and stimulating, the arts can touch buried sensitivities in the dullest minds and careless hearts in ways beyond the capacity of any form of the mass media.

A murder recorded in a newspaper is now almost a commonplace occurrence, quickly read and quickly forgotten; the reader does not identify with the victim or have much empathy with the people involved. But a murder portrayed in drama or literature can create intense feelings of horror and injustice. Crime statistics may be disturbing, but to see violent crime enacted on stage, or on the technicolour screen, is infinitely more distressing. Six million Jews being murdered by the Nazi régime is almost beyond the imagination, but to read a novel about the treatment of one Jew in Nazi Germany is to realise something of the full horror of the six million.

In our technological century the dehumanisation of the individual has been a steady progress which we are conditioned to take as normal. But the reality is brought home to us when we see, with shock and apprehension, the artist's vision of modern man; an individual turned into a machine, a faceless creature where the things that make him unique are destroyed. We may blindly accept, or ignore, the chaos of contemporary worldviews where nothing makes sense, but when this absurdity is worked out on stage or in music, the effect can be shattering.

Not only can the arts extend our experience by bringing universal truth onto a personal level, but they can powerfully reveal our own hearts to ourselves. As Hamlet said

> The play's the thing
> Wherein I'll catch the conscience of the King. (4)

So he used the art of drama, not only to show the King that others knew of his murderous action, but to rouse the 'conscience of the King'. It was a means of showing the King himself in a dramatic and truthful way.

In some of the enacted sermons of the Prophets, and in the telling of parables, this method is used in the Bible. The most obvious example is the story Nathan recounted to David in 2 Samuel 12. Nathan told a story about a poor man who had a lamb, his only possession, and how a rich and powerful neighbour took the lamb. When David was angry at hearing of such injustice, Nathan completed the story with the assertion, 'You are that man'. It was then that David suffered the 'shock of recognition', seeing the sinfulness of his own actions in seducing Bathsheba and arranging for her husband to be killed.

This 'shock of recognition' is a common experience when confronted by true works of art. We suddenly recognise something as true, are aware our own heart testifies to its truth, yet in a strange way we have never been aware of its truth before. We are seeing our own heart, and seeing the truth, in a way which previously seemed to be beyond our own experience. The arts can pierce the veil of our own complacency and awaken what is in our own hearts.

There is a sense in which much contemporary art is rejected for this very reason. Modern arts can be disturbing and frightening where they reveal the spiritual poverty of the age, showing the disorientation and desolation of 20th-century man in a world where harmony, beauty and meaning seem to have disappeared. Perhaps they are showing ourselves to ourselves and the truth can indeed be uncomfortable.

As well as extending the reality of experience and emotions, the arts have a function to perform in exploring all the realms of created order.

Exploring Creation

It is a calling of the arts to explore creation, to examine and disclose the wonderful, beautiful and yet terrible, world of objects, animals and plants, as well as people with their tangled emotions, fears, hopes and thoughts mingled with the infinite longings of the human heart. The artist, in his unique way, can unfold to some measure the true place of man in the world and his relationship to God and all created things. No matter where the artist probes, the farthest reaches of outer space or deep into the human psyche, all is part of the creation of God.

The task of the artist in exploring and disclosing is not the same as the calling of science. The artist's role is not to catalogue or classify individual aspects of the creational structure, nor to analyse materials or events in order to formulate tentative theories of a rational kind. The tools of the artist are imagination and insight, intuition and creative thinking, and then the craftsmanship to make his vision a reality of communication to others.

His task is to discover, so that all may enjoy, the richness of creation. Its diversity yet its essential unity; its continual change yet its solid per-manancy; its complexity and yet its basic simplicity; its wonder and its glory. The arts can do all this, leading to a greater appreciation of the wonders of creation.

As a Dutch scholar once said: "Art reveals ordinances of creation which neither science, nor politics, nor religious life, nor even revelation can bring to light." (5)

They can make us aware of the infinity of space or the beauty of a single leaf. Nothing is too great or too small for art. In this way the artist can give us awareness and teach us how to look at things. Oscar Wilde once remarked that 'nature always copies art'; as with so many of Wilde's epigrams, there is here an element of truth.

If we occasionally visit Art Galleries and take an interest in landscapes, it is most likely when walking in the country we will be looking at the surrounding scenery with added interest, even comparing it with the paintings we know. Cloud formations on a painting will encourage us to look at the clouds overhead and even a still life of a bowl of fruit will help us to look intensely, and appreciate the sheen and beauty to be found on the skin of an apple or grape. Nature appears to be copying art.

It can be asked if the Lake District in the north of England would have been as popular a tourist attraction if the Lake Poets had never existed. Although it had always been a place of rugged grandeur it took the artist to reveal its beauty so that others, through poetry and painting, could learn the value for themselves.

What happens, of course, is that the artist isolates a moment of time, selects a particular view, or examines a specific situation, and by his skill makes us concentrate our attention on it. He makes us look, teaching us to observe, showing us the things we have often ignored or forgotten.

There is a need for such art in the present age; an art that will take all of creation for its provenance. Materialism has cut man off from the spiritual realm and affluence has corrupted a true sense of values. It is the age of reductionism which has reduced man, and the whole created order; many faiths and philosophies are contributing to the process.

Capitalism has reduced man to a consumer; Marxism reduces him to a mere economic unit; the behavioural sciences reduce him to the status of a programmed computer; existentialism, in all its branches, reduces him to his own experience; modern philosophy reduces all things to language, and many Christians have reduced even salvation to a private and personalised emotion. The artist, by his very calling, must be the enemy of reductionism by revealing the greatness of creation and man who was made to be its steward.

In exposing and disclosing all things the arts must also show the limitations that are within creation. When a dramatist shows the fall of a man who tried to be a god he is revealing the limitations within the created order – man cannot be as God. When a painter portrays what people look like when they no longer believe that they are creatures made in the image of God then he is exposing the reality of creation – if man is not the image bearer of God then he is an accidental nothing. The deliberate distorting of sounds, and the search for non-human music created by chance, does help to show that without rational harmony and purpose human life must be painful and meaningless.

Then there is the existence of evil; the fact that sin has invaded the good world that God made. So the true artist cannot have a rosy, romantic picture of reality. Exploring creation means a search for the truth. Here arises an apparent paradox.

"Art is a lie which makes us realise the truth," (6) said Picasso. Art reveals aspects of the truth by telling lies; it consists of fictions and illusions and its power lies in the fact that we submit to the illusion and accept the fiction.

When sitting in a theatre an audience is aware that the characters on stage are really different from what they appear; they are actors playing a part, not expressing their own emotions but reciting words they have memorised. Yet the audience submit to the illusion and become involved with the conflict and events being enacted on the stage. If a character dies on stage, no one is astonished to see him walking about later; it is accepted he did not really die although the scene may have brought tears.

It is the same in a novel or poem; it may be fiction but readers become emotionally involved, as if experiencing the agony of real people in real situations. A painting may move us deeply although we are aware it is simply pigment on canvas. The arts are a lie which can make us realise truth. Without being real they disclose reality in an intense and unique way. This is because they have their own language speaking to the human heart.

Expanding Language

The arts have given mankind another language to explore their experience, emotions and all of creation. This language can be a medium of truth.

To be true to reality does not mean that all art must be representational art. In fact art is never a copy of reality and cannot be an exact imitation of real life. Art is always selection and interpretation.

The landscapes of Constable are not mirror images of the scene; his sketchbooks show how he experimented with different settings for trees and buildings to suit his purpose and create the right balance which he sought.

The dialogue of a play, no matter how realistic it may sound, can never be a precise copy of everyday speech but a careful selection of words to give the impression of everyday speech. This is why the 'kitchen sink' drama movement of a few years ago failed – real, everyday conversation is vague, inconsequential and lacking structure; it seldom has direction or tension. In a novel, no matter how natural or realistic it may seem, the events are always a selection and interpretation compared to real life where incidents and events occur in an apparently chaotic and illogical fashion.

So no matter his medium, the artist attempting to show reality must always select and manipulate his material. He blends it together according to his imaginative perception and his ability to speak directly to other imaginations. This means that it is not to the rational, logical part of man that art first makes its appeal; it communicates directly to the heart and the imagination. The painting, play, novel, poem, or piece of music can have a power which supercedes critical and rational faculties; these may later be brought in to make a critical assessment, but the initial impact is at the deepest level of heart and mind. The arts can do this not by physical reality, but by the powerful language of myths and symbols – a potent language indeed.

The power of symbols is seen in the importance that is attached to them, even in daily life. A wedding ring itself is only a strip of gold to be worn on the finger, but to define it as such is to reduce it to mere decoration or an item of no great value. But in our culture, and especially to a young bride or groom, it is an object of great significance. It is a symbol worth far more than its intrinsic value. Equally a flag is merely a piece of coloured cloth and the National Anthem of a nation is simply a well-known tune; but, as symbols, they have far more meaning and more deeply valued connotations.

Allied to symbols is ritual – symbolic actions. In all the great, and not so great, events of life certain rituals are performed. At birth, birthdays, holidays, marriage, death, we perform certain motions and act in certain ways – rituals are always appropriate to the event. Here in Scotland the traditional Hogmanay behaviour in 'first-footing' – carrying coal, shortbread, a bottle – is all ritualistic. Even lifting a hat to a lady, saluting or shaking hands are all symbolic actions which seem part of life.

Myths speak directly to the heart. So the folk music, songs and stories of a culture are more than pleasant little tunes or tales; they can be the race memory of a nation. So a man, born and brought up in Glasgow, will respond to a song of the Hebrides even although he has never been there and perhaps has no desire to visit them.

The artist is the maker of dreams, the forger of symbols and the creator of myths. But these must be seen for what they are, languages that are pointing to a greater reality. If the myth or symbol is seen, or accepted, as true in itself, then the reality it is seeking to reveal becomes obscure, if not lost. If in *The Plague*, it is taken that Albert Camus is simply telling a story of what happens in a city in the grip of a bubonic plague then it has nothing to say about the human condition. If *Animal Farm* by George Orwell is taken as a fairy tale then it has no satirical value or anything to teach about the uses of political power. The arts must point to something outside of themselves and the image must never be taken as the reality.

3

ART AND LIFE

Some years ago an exhibition of the works of Picasso was held in Glasgow Art Gallery and aroused a great deal of interest. One of the city newspapers published a cartoon showing a man rushing from the gallery shouting, "Let me out, I'm beginning to like them!"

This cartoon illustrates the immediate reaction of ordinary people when faced with something beyond their comprehension; they either laugh or react in fear. There can be little doubt that most people, when confronted with contemporary art, find it incomprehensible and strangely disturbing. Modern music, dance, drama, poetry, painting and literature do tend to confuse and perplex.

But this suspicion of the arts is not confined to contemporary productions. The 'arts' – in all their disciplines – with their capital letters and connotations of superiority, are considered as suitable only for the select few. They are seen as far removed from the real experience of daily living. So theatre, orchestral concert and ballet are minority interests. Art galleries are not places of mass viewing. Poetry, apart from the 'Burns' season' here in Scotland, is not widely read and the classical novels are considered more for those studying English Literature than for reading for pleasure and enlightenment.

"I know nothing about art but I know what I like" is more than a cliché or confession of ignorance. Often it is defensive arrogance. It is a recognition that we can respond to certain artistic expressions and are not totally lacking in aesthetic appreciation. There is truth in this; the arts are a gift of God to mankind and all men have the capacity to appreciate the highest forms of craftsmanship. Indeed, art is not only in all of life but is part of life.

In All of Life

We cannot escape the arts. In every sphere of life we are confronted with art; it affects our homes, environment and personal lifestyles, and dominates our social experience. We are all influenced by the art forms of the age and are children of a common artistic heritage. The artist is not confined to the art gallery nor the dramatist to the theatre; the novelist is not imprisoned in the library nor the musician in the concert hall; the arts are a subtle force surrounding daily living. They are expressed in homes, places of work and recreation, streets and cities, and even in places of worship.

In homes the décor, furniture and furnishings, all reflect some artistic style. Our bedrooms are normally painted or papered in quiet pastel shades with curtains of floral or abstract design to match the carpet and bedspread. Pictures, probably reproductions of flowers or a still life, will decorate the blank expanse of the walls and ornaments will be tastefully arranged on the dressing table.

In the living room we are scarcely conscious of the artistic designs and patterns on the carpets, curtains, chairs and walls or the shape and texture of the ornaments and objects with which we surround ourselves. At mealtimes we will hardly notice the delicate patterns on the china dishes, the design of the pottery or the shape and engraving on the cutlery.

All around us, in our homes, are colours, patterns, forms, designs and artistic artefacts. Most of them may be considered the 'applied arts' rather than the 'fine arts' but in taking art to be a craft the difference is one of degree and not of kind. All aspects of art add a rich dimension to family life and are necessary to make a house into a home expressing the views, tastes and values of the tenant.

Outside the home we again come face to face with the arts in their many forms. There are tower blocks, houses and buildings of all shapes and purposes designed for a specific need yet becoming part of the environment and having an effect on the people using or seeing them. Architecture is an artistic expression which shapes our towns and affects our view of man and society.

All around our communities are examples of art. Apart from statues and memorials, there are billboards and neon adverts carrying vivid messages with distinctive images and lettering to make the greatest impact. Many shops have raised window dressing almost to a high art and even the packaging of food and materials are now designed to be aesthetically pleasing and psychologically attractive.

Even Church buildings are artistically designed to help the worship of God. It may be a building of towering spire and Gothic majesty, or custom-built to suit the economics of the present age, but it will have an impact and influence on the people gathered there. Huge pillars and arches will dwarf the people, making them conscious of their smallness and insignificance before God; a custom-designed building, more common in our age perhaps because it corresponds to modern's man's idea of himself with everything cut down to his size, will have its effect on his religious and emotional experience. Churches, even the most modern, are not complex designs with garish colours, but usually basically simple with restful quiet shades to help sustain a mood of reverence and peace.

Even in a service of worship we cannot escape the arts. Apart from the works of the craftsmen in the physical building there are art forms employed in the conduct of public worship. In most church services there is music, poetry or ritual in some form or other. Organists play voluntaries, choirs sing, and all the congregation sing psalms or hymns – which are essentially poems set to music. Readings will be given, most probably in the matchless prose of the Authorised version of the Bible, and in the prayers and sermon there will be rhetoric and literary devices used. No matter how non-liturgical the service may be there will still be employed a certain degree of symbolism and ritual. The arts are part of worship.

The arts are in all of life, in our homes, social environment and even in our worship. We are exposed to them in television, radio, books, newspapers, magazines and all the facets of modern life. But they are not only surrounding us, they are part of our humanness.

As Part of Life

The arts are a necessity of life. Both individual and corporate life would be infintely impoverished if there were no art to add beauty, colour, harmony and new dimensions to human experience.

Plato argued that "the object of education is to teach us to love beauty." (1) But the desire for, and the love of, beauty does not come solely through education; it is part of man's nature. Perhaps the longing for loveliness and beauty is part of the race memory of the lost Eden man was made to dwell in. Real beauty does carry a hint of sadness, a vague nostalgia for something lost; perhaps it carries echoes of the glory that was lost through the Fall.

Just as we respond when confronted with beauty so we find that all the arts have their own pecular effect upon us. These often appear to transcend rational understanding. The myths of a nation are often more influential in our thinking than its actual history, and images seem to have such latent properties that most people would feel uncomfortable at tearing up photos of a loved one. Music is a powerful force in creating emotions and drama has been recognised, since Aristotle, as a means of purging the soul with 'terror and pity'. Even colours affect us; some bring warmth and comfort while others make us feel cold and uncomfortable.

A group of volunteers once sat down to a meal under special lighting conditions. The use of these lights altered the natural colours of the various foods so that the milk appeared blood red, the potatoes blue and the meat green. While this had little effect on a few the majority found the food to be repulsive and some became physically sick. Yet the food was natural, only the colours had been changed.

It is not that we simply respond to the arts; they are part of life, all men have a measure of creativity. Indeed it is men and women alone who are the creatures of creativity. Rabbits do not decorate their burrows; birds do not place ornaments in their nests; monkeys do not try to surround themselves with beauty; owls do not sing in praise of the moon and dogs cannot sing a love song. Animals can only act according to their God-given instincts; man alone is free to create and develop new things and all men and women have a measure of this gift. The creativity of the artist and the creativity of the ordinary person differ only in degree; all are not equally gifted but all have the gift.

As Calvin wrote: "But although all are not equally able to learn all the arts we have sufficient evidence of a common capacity in the fact that there is scarcely an individual who does not display intelligence in some particular art. And this capacity extends not merely to the learning of the art, but to the devising of something new, or the improving of what has been previously learned." (2)

So men will plant flowers in a garden, not in an unthinking profusion, but carefully to ensure a colourful and harmonious pattern. A woman, even with no artistic training, will spend time arranging a vase of flowers into a pleasing arrangement. Children will delight in chanting a meaningless alliterative phrase that has appealed to them. They are all using the creativity within them; responding with an innate sense of wonder and appreciation at what can be done with colour, shapes and sounds.

Albert Camus tells of a man who created a world of beauty and harmony behind bars. A German prisoner of war, imprisoned in a Russian Labour Camp, collected small pieces of wood and nailed them to the edge of a table to make a dummy piano keyboard. At night he would sit happily playing this dummy keyboard. With eyes closed he would finger the keys, listening with the ears of imagination to the music he was creating in his own mind. This man was using his God-given faculties, enjoying, through memory and imagination, the transcendant pleasures and reality of the art of music. He was reminding himself that harmony and beauty are still part of what it means to be human, even in a world where these things appeared to have been destroyed.

In unexpected places the creativity of man breaks through. In one of the hydro-electric stations in the North of Scotland there is a generating hall where the air throbs with power and strength as the whirling generators create energy and men are seldom seen. It is a place of technical efficiency where technology works on its own and men are unnecessary. But, in this particular hydro-electric station, lined along the wall of the generating'hall, there is a row of flowering plants. Someone has taken the trouble to bring these flowers inside, to tend and care for them, so that they could add beauty and colour to an otherwise sterile atmosphere. Whoever brought and tended these plants was acting in response to a God-given impulse to add loveliness and a bright richness to the drabbest of surroundings. It was a creative act.

This creativity and innate desire for form, meaning and beauty, is one of the reasons why industrial and commercial design has now reached a high degree of artistic professionalism. It is a reaction to an age when so much contemporary art is formless and fragmented beauty and design is being emphasised. While much modern art may be meant to disturb it is being unthinkingly rejected; people do not accept, or appreciate, paintings without apparent form or meaning; the torturing noises of the avant garde. composers; word spinning of the absurd dramatists, or irrational poetry or literature. The old concepts of harmony and beauty are being destroyed but mankind cannot live without them. So to satisfy this demand, ordinary objects are now made as items of beauty.

It can be seen in the sleek streamlining of the modern motor car; in the simple harmony of a modern plane such as Concorde; in the uncluttered elegance of modern ships and yachts and the deceptively frail dignity of modern bridges. The designers, who are craftsmen in the true meaning of the word, have reduced lines and patterns to the bare minimum and created something pleasing to the eye. But not only in large artefacts and machines are the designs aesthetically pleasing; the same is generally true of the everyday objects of common life. Some modern cutlery, with its rigid symmetry and yet delicate flowing lines, is almost a work of art in itself. Pots and pans; dishes and vases; covers and cushions; chairs and tables; household goods and clothes are shaped and designed to appeal to a sense of beauty as well as to serve a utilitarian purpose.

The high degree of artistic work being shown in contemporary design reveals something that would appear to have been forgotten in much modern art. Shapelessness is not an artistic form and lack of meaning should not be mistaken for originality.

By the very nature of his work, the designer must be disciplined. He is compelled to work with clearly defined and finely restricted limits. A man making a motor car, or a jam spoon, cannot let his imagination fly unrestricted and seek to create something totally new and original. He is forced by the fact that the object must serve a practical purpose to accept strict limitations in what he can do. Rather than inhibiting a true artist or craftsman, this calls for a greater degree of creative and disciplined imagination. This acceptance of limitations would appear to be lost in much of the contemporary artistic scene..

Art is part of life because it is part of what it means to be human. Indeed there is no part of life where God-given creativity and a desire for harmony and beauty does not have influence.

Even in Science

Even apparently objective activities such as mathematics and scientific research are affected and influenced by aesthetic factors. In their writings scientists often refer to the harmony, simplicity, elegance and beauty that they find in their researches and theories. The norms of art are not absent from their considerations.

Einstein said of Isaac Newton that he combined, in himself, the experimenter, the theorist, the mechanic and, 'not least, the artist'. Another scientist, Hinshelwood, once argued that chemistry was not only a mental discipline but an adventure and an 'aesthetic experience'.

Even the coldly logical structure of mathematics has this aesthetic element. Bertrand Russell, who did so much work in mathematics, logic and philosophy, wrote: "Mathematics possesses not only truth, but supreme beauty — a beauty cold and austere, like that of sculpture, without appeal to any part of our weaker nature, sublimely pure and capable of a stern perfection such as only the greatest art can show." (3)

So even the scientist, in approaching his calling and work, is not devoid of a sense of the beautiful and harmonious. He responds to these facets of life as much as any other man. Indeed they can govern his outlook and findings.

Albert Einstein was once given a theory to consider; it was a detailed hypothesis which was meant to account for all the known facts in a certain field of study. Rather to the surprise of the scientist who had worked on, and formulated, the theory, Einstein handed it back with the comment, 'it is not beautiful enough'. Truth and beauty are often related.

The arts are a necessity which are in every sphere of life and no one, scientist, mathematician or layman, can escape the human desire to satisfy the aesthetic norms which God has placed in the human heart. They are part of God's creation, part of our creaturehood and humanity. Not only do they affect all of life but are part of what it means to be truly human.

PART TWO

THE CONTEMPORARY SCENE

4

THE ARTS TODAY

True art, in whatever medium, has a timeless quality. The tortured conscience and vacillation of a Hamlet can be understood without any comprehension of Elizabethan England; the paintings of Rembrandt can be appreciated without any knowledge of 17th-century Holland, and the enjoyment of classical music does not depend upon a knowledge of 18th- or 19th-century history. When the arts reflect something of the human heart and reveal facets of the great, beautiful and yet fearsome reality of life they are dealing with universals which are true of the human condition in all ages. The arts can, and should, transcend their age and achieve a timeless quality for all generations.

But the artist is a child of his age. The idea of the lone romantic genius starving in his garret, untouched and untroubled by his age, may be attractive but remains a myth. By the very nature of man and society the artist is conditioned by the values and culture of his society. He is not removed from the reality of the socio-cultural climate or the dominant philosophies of his age. Because of his gifts, insights and intuitions, he may be able to dream dreams and see beyond as well as behind his age, but he is still part of the world into which he was born. He is still a child of his culture.

While the true artist is a child of his culture it is also true that the culture is a child of the artist. There is always an interaction between the arts and the age. Society may help to mould the artist but the artist, in turn, helps to shape the community and culture of which he is part. So whether the arts are reinforcing, or rebelling against the values and ethos of an age they are not remote from the real world.

In the real world of the 20th century the arts have been responding and protesting to the pressures, forces and powers let loose on the age. It has been an age of lost dreams, lost men and the shattered mirror of the arts seeking to reflect the true nature of contemporary reality.

Lost Dreams

It has been a century of lost dreams. In Europe there have been two wars of such terrifying proportion that two generations, within a quarter of a centurey, died on the ever-expanding battlefields. The comfortable optimism of the Victorian and Edwardian years died violently upon the battlefields of Europe and has been buried beneath the growing realisation of the brilliant aptitude of man to create ever greater weapons of destruction. The hope underlying the scientific romances of the early Wells has given way to the technological nightmare of Huxley's *Brave New World*; the dream of the Romantic and Socialist poets has ended with the nightmare of 1984. Utopianism seems strangely old-fashioned today.

In addition to war there is the growth of other, equally frightening problems. A growing lawlessness affecting every sphere of society, and the rise of urban terrorism. Vandalism and crime appear to be growing to epidemic proportions as the old moralities disappear. Industrialisation has bequeathed the problems of diminishing resources, pollution, cycles of over production and recessions and apparent economic chaos. Whatever view is taken of our age — post-Christian or the dawn of a new era — it is a peculiarly grey age. A dream turning into a nightmare can only bring darkness.

In many ways it is an age without colour. In spite of fluorescent print, psychedelic patterns and the 'living colour' of the television screen, it is a grey world. Most people are compelled to live out their lives in the urban sprawl of the great cities, either in decaying areas of former architectural beauty, or in the characterless concrete boxes of the new housing estates. Streets have been turned on end and families neatly filed away in tower blocks where loneliness has replaced community and social life has become fragmented and artificial.

The greyness is seen, not only in the decaying or rebuilt cities, new towns, towers and motorways, but on the faces of those who never look upwards except on the sun-worshipping sprees of annual holidays. The heavens declare the glory of God but the stars cannot be seen for the sodium lights on the man-made streets.

Daily work, which should bring its own satisfaction and sense of achievement, has been largely reduced to a meaningless monotony; a depersonalising and dehumanising activity. Or the economic demands of the productive process means that machines must replace men, leaving them to idle life away on the streets of a 'society that has no need of their gifts or services. Instead of rejoicing in useful, fulfilling lives in a world of beauty and splendour, the majority exist in a multiplicity of Babels where even the flowers and trees wilt in the polluted air.

As one European thinker has put it: "Men now live in conditions that are less than human. Consider the concentration of our great cities, the slums, the lack of space, of air, of time, the gloomy streets and sallow lights that confuse night and day. Think of our dehumanised factories, our unsatisfied senses, our working women, our estrangement from nature. Life in such an environment has no meaning. Consider our public transportation in which a man is less important than a parcel; our hospitals, in which he is only a number. Yet we call this progress . . .. And the noise, that monster boring into us at every hour of the day and night without respite." (1)

Life is grey, dull, monotonous and meaningless for the vast majority of people compelled to live in a one-dimensional world. A world of mass production and throw-away goods and where the only dream is that of escape. So they retreat into the world of illusion where the trivia of television and transistorised music helps to keep thought and reality at bay.

The young stupify their senses with deafening music, drug themselves with alcohol, nicotine, soft or hard drugs and reject a society they do not understand and which, apparently, does not understand them. The old retreat into the loneliness of their homes and seek companionship with the only company they have — friendly faces on a cathode tube, while those in the long years between youth and age search for colour and excitement in the plastic luxury of club, pub or bingo hall; or they puruse riches and possessions that give the false promise of the 'good life'.

It is an age that needs the arts. Not the soporific mass arts of the media where illusion makes a pretence to reality and does not enhance or enrich life but provides merely a momentary escape. What is desperately needed is an art that will truly show the poverty of the age while asserting there is more to life than plastic baubles; that there is no profit in gaining the whole world of technological gadgets and losing your own soul. What is needed is an art which will face the reality of the 20th century, with its material progress and spiritual recession, its vaunted independence and grey conformity, and show that there is more to life than prosperity and escape. As a Persian poet of the 13th century put it:

> If of thy mortal goods thou art bereft,
> And from thy slender store two loaves alone to thee are left,
> Sell one, and with the dole
> Buy hyacinths to feed thy soul. (2)

But there is so little in contemporary art to feed the soul. The arts too seem caught in a one dimensional world, often revealing the basic deprivation of the age but having nothing to say beyond a wail of existential despair. As Ionesco, one of the leading European dramatists, has confessed: "The art of today is by and large a storeroom, a museum of our despair." (3)

The problem for the arts as well as for all of life, is that in a materialistic culture there is no room for God and therefore no spiritual reality. Science, technology, politics, economics, sociology, philosophy and all aspects of modern culture seem to function without any reference to God; the arts and media appear to thrive and prosper without any need, or acknowledgement, of the Living God. Into the very bones of modern man has come the feeling that God has nothing to do with the 20th century. Man must face and conquer all his own problems.

But, having in his own mind, banished God from the universe, man now finds himself in a world that does not make sense. He is unsure of his place and role in creation. History has no understandable beginning and can have no conceivable end; life at an individual level has no significance. In an infinite universe, human life must remain small, finite and inexplicable.

With the departure of God from the thought life of the culture, more than the biblical God has disappeared; man, as an individual, has also faded away.

Lost Man

Erich Fromm, the modern psychologist, has asserted: "In the 19th century the problem was that God was dead; in the 20th century the problem is that man is dead. In the 19th century inhumanity meant cruelty; in the 20th century it means schizoid self-alienation. The danger of the past was that men became slaves. The danger of the future is that they become robots." (4)

In place of the individual, unique and made in the image of God, has come the mass man of the mass age. Man the faceless cog of the technologically-organised society of the 20th century. Modern man does not exist as an individual.

He is merged into great cities, educated in large schools and colleges in a conveyer-belt system of education to produce faceless technicians for the technical society. All his life takes place in the mass. He is employed in national, or multinational, combines and protected by membership of massive trade unions. Mass circulation newspapers inform, the mass media entertain, and increasingly there is little room for the individual. In every area of life — even in church — this is true. Small congregations must be merged into larger, more economic units. In all of life the individual is being driven into the mass man of the mass age.

It is also the age of mass art forms for the mass man. In cinema, radio and television, the work is not done by one highly gifted individual but by the many trained technicians who understand and can manipulate the media. In cinema there are scriptwriters, producers, directors, cameramen, production assistants and many more involved in the making of a film. It may be true that the ultimate responsibility lies with the director, but the finished film is the sum total of many efforts and is only possible through the work of many men and women. Radio, because of the intimacy of the medium, may depend more upon the actual writer or composer for the success of any particular programme, but television has had to follow the film industry with its team of experts to produce a programme. Even in live theatre the trend has been towards more people being involved in each production so that it becomes a group effort. The day of the actor-manager producing his own play seems to have gone.

Mass art must be global in its approach and popular in its treatment of any theme. Films and television programmes are made for mass distribution so, rather than aiming at any particular culture, they reflect the lowest common denominator. A long succession of bland Hollywood films were made which did not reflect a truly American view but, with an eye on the European market, a 'mid-Atlantic' culture that was false to both sides of the ocean. Equally, many British films have included American actors, not for artistic or dramatic purposes, but to help in getting distribution rights in the United States.

On a national level, radio and television have had the same effect. Some programmes have tried to treat seriously the differing cultures in the regions, but there is the temptation, not always resisted, of being patronising. Local cultures are often treated as quaint and primitive customs that have surprisingly survived into our internationally sophisticated age. The ignoring of local cultures must end by destroying them.

Man was made to live in fellowship with God and in community. If God has departed and truly human communities are disappearing then meaning has departed from individual life. Perhaps contemporary artists are facing the agony of this more than most. They are confronting the intuitive dread that lies in the hearts of all men; that we are living meaningless lives in a meaningless universe. It is clear in all the arts how the place of man in the universe has changed over the centuries.

Shakespeare could write: "What a piece of work is man! How noble in reason! How infinite in faculties! In form and moving, how express and admirable! In action how like an angel! In apprehension how like a god! The beauty of the world! The paragon of animals!" (5)

Such a view of man can be found celebrated in the prose, poetry and music of the past centuries. The artist's vision of him as strong, noble and dignified, can be seen in the sculptures and paintings of the art galleries. Man was indeed seen as only 'a little lower than the angels'.

When we come to our age, however, we find: "There is a painful irony in the new image of man that is emerging, however fragmentarily, from the art of our time. . . . . If an observer from Mars were to turn his attention from the external appurtenances of power to the shape of man revealed in our novels, plays, paintings and sculpture, he would find there a creature full of holes and gaps, faceless, riddled with doubts and negations, starkly finite." (6)

The arts, and philosophy, reveal a radically different view of man from that shown in Scripture or in the arts of the past. Indeed the very question 'what is man?' has become almost meaningless as it has become compounded by the specialist approach of biologist, psychologist, sociologist, anthropologist and philosopher. Only the theological word 'lost' can truly express the contemporary condition of man.

But certainly the arts of our day show man as a faceless, formless, entity struggling to express his identity. A creature seemingly little more than a 'useless passion', incapable of true communication. He is facing the reality of nothingness.

This is the horror that underlies almost all the work of Franz Kafka. His characters are real, they are placed in apparently real situations, yet the reality does not make sense. Full comprehension is always frustrated and ultimate meaning cannot be found. In his novel, *The Castle*, a land surveyor, known simply as K, has been promised a position by the inhabitants of a mysterious castle. K finds himself caught in a bureaucratic and hierarchical structure that makes communication complicated, and indeed impossible. He cannot find what he has to do.

Another novel, *The Trial* the story is of a man, again simply known as K, who is arrested by some mysterious authority and accused of unknown crimes. Again there is the problem of communication K does not know who has arrested him, what precise charges are being made against him, or who is his judge. He only knows constant frustration as he fruitlessly seeks justice. It all ends with him being destroyed as a human being with status and dignity and he 'dies like a dog'.

These novels, with the other works of Kafka, are more than prophetic disclosures of the condition of modern man caught in the bureaucratic maze of the technological world. They go much deeper and can be seen as allegories of the contemporary human condition. Modern man, like man of all ages, has been made to serve God. But today he cannot reach the Castle to find his calling and task; burdened with a guilt he does not understand he cannot find divine justice.

As Kafka himself has written: "What is sin? . . . . We know the word and the practice, but the sense and knowledge of sin has been lost. Perhaps that is itself damnation. God-forsakenness, meaninglessness." (7)

Perhaps the very irrationality, the sheer meaninglessness of much modern art is a real reflection of the meaningless world of the 20th century. The arts can reflect the real world by holding a mirror up to nature.

Broken Mirror

It was Shakespeare who coined the phrase of a 'mirror to nature'. He put the words into Hamlet's mouth, giving the reason for the play. "The purpose of playing, whose end, both at the first and now, was and is, to hold, as 'twere, the mirror up to nature." (8)

The arts of the age can be a mirror reflecting what is true in society and culture. But to look at the arts of the contemporary scene is to see distortion and fragmentation. The mirror seems to be shattered, giving a confused and complicated view without the comfort of a pattern.

Certainly to explore the arts of the 20th century is to venture into a strange land where all the signposts and landmarks are gone. That they appear to have been deliberately destroyed only adds to the sense of disorientation and desolation. It is to engage in a pursuit down a Kafkaesque corridor leading nowhere, with doors attractive and repulsive, opening out into various degrees of darkness. The arts seem to be on a journey without destination.

The fervour of experimentation in all the arts reflects more than the pace of change in the modern world. It is an attempt to mend the mirror of the arts. So the 20th century, in painting, has seen Neo-impressionalism and Post-impressionalism; there have been Abstract, Expressionalism, Dadaism, Cubism, Pop and Op art and Photorealism. In drama there have been the Natural Theatre, Epic Theatre, the Theatre of Commitment, Living Theatre, the Theatre of the Absurd and the Theatre of Cruelty. Literature has produced novels and anti-novels with heroes and anti-heroes. Musicians have sought new scales and new sounds while poetry has become more obscure with unknown images and often lack of chronological narrative. There is apparently no end to the experiments in finding new expressions, techniques and art-forms that will reflect the reality of the age and speak to contemporary man.

Much of the art produced today is the result of a deeply-felt anguish at the horror of being in a world where meaning has departed and there appears to be no hope. That is why so many contemporary expressions of the arts are concerned with questions of guilt, identity, meaning and the search for authentic existence. Modern man is helpless and through his art his loneliness, his alienation, and his disintegration as a human being can be seen. The dominance of the erotic and the growing fascination with violence show something of man striving to assert his essential humanity.

Playwrights such as Miller, Albee, Becket, Osborne, Pinter and Ionesco often brilliantly, and sometimes unforgettably, present the human dilemma, but in the final analysis, they have no answer. All that can be suggested is the existential 'nobility in the face of absurdity'. They are men of our age speaking to our age.

The same is true of the painters, sculptors, musicians, novelists and poets. They are revealing with intense vision and sensitivity the horror and pain of the contemporary world. It is too easy, and a false judgement, to dismiss all modern art as cheap attempts to gain noteriety or financial success. As in all fields there are undoubtedly many charlatans who hide the poverty of their craftsmanship by undisciplined work. But many dedicated, honest and highly-gifted artists are striving to present artistic statements of the highest integrity. What they reveal may be disturbing, perplexing and disconcerting but a mirror cannot be condemned for the picture it reflects.

The fact that much contemporary art may be meant to disturb means that most people reject it without analysing the motives or rationalising their reaction. It is the instinctive reaction of those who do not want to be reminded of their poverty. A challenge ignored or a question unheard cannot be a valid response to any artistic statement.

So we find rich stockbrokers applaud plays where capitalism is attacked; logicians praise absurd art, and decent people mistake blasphemy and obscenity for profundity. The masses find escape from their spiritual poverty in the trivial laughter of canned amusement. It is not surprising that serious artists often turn in upon themselves, writing or creating for other artists as they see their vision being treated as 'entertaining' or 'interesting'.

But the Christian cannot so easily escape the challenge of the arts or the world. An understanding of the arts will lead to a better understanding of the world of the 20th century; the world of lost dreams, lost men and broken images. As the arts protest and seek refuge in a new form of mysticism it is the task of the Christian to listen, to try and understand, and then to seek to bring the healing of the cross to the bruised body of the contemporary arts.

5

THE AGONY OF PROTEST

At the heart of much contemporary art lies a deep-rooted protest which is more intense than the arts of previous centuries ever showed. Although not often considered in relation to the arts, protest has long been an attractive theme for artists. Some of the greatest art and literature has come from strong feelings of outrage against some form of injustice.

The artist Goya, with his fellow liberals, welcomed Napoleon's invasion of Spain thinking it would bring justice and freedom; instead it brought ruthless brutality and the needless slaughter of innocent people. He expressed his protest and horror in a series of etchings, 'The Disasters of War' which depict the suffering of the people. In his painting, 'The Executions of May 3, 1808' he revealed in stark agony the execution of poor victims facing their death. The peasants being executed seem to be the only real human beings in the picture, they stand with terror-stricken faces while the firing squad are in a neat line, faces hidden, so that they appear merely military uniforms and rifles carrying out orders.

More recently there was the bitter statement of protest by Picasso in his 'Guernica', named after the Spanish city destroyed by German bombers during the civil war. It is a powerful picture, full of intense imagery in black, grey and white tones with the distorted and fragmented figures of men, women, children and animals all screaming in pain and terror.

Literature has also been used in protest. Many of the novels of Charles Dickens are not only great literature and characterisation but also searing indictments against the social conditions of the Victorian age. In America, *Uncle Tom's Cabin*, was not simply a popular novel but a tract against slavery first serialised in an anti-slave journal. Upton Sinclair's novel, *The Jungle*, led to new laws in America dealing with the preparation of food and, in France, Emile Zola used fiction as social protest. The First World War produced the agonised protest of the war poets expressing their shock and disgust in the mud-filled trenches as a war to save civilisation was fought with the fury of barbarians.

There has certainly been much to protest about in this century, and many forms of artistic protest. Evelyn Waugh and the early Aldous Huxley satirised brilliantly the fashionable intellectual set of the twenties and Shaw used the stage as a vehicle of protest. Huxley and Orwell protested in the anti-Utopian novels, *Brave New World* and *1984*. In our own age we have seen the era of protest songs and poetry and there are still left wing drama groups presenting plays as a protest against the evils of capitalism.

But much contemporary art raises its voice against more than social cruelty or political injustice. There is a genuine protest against the whole ethos of 20th century life; an expression of a deeply-felt anguish of the dilemma of man in the modern world. The agony of protest is all the more real because the old answers no longer make sense and the old certainties have disappeared.

Martin Esslin, who is currently head of BBC Radio Drama, has written: "There can be little doubt that such a sense of disillusionment, such a collapse of previously held firm beliefs is a characteristic feature of our time . . .. There can be no doubt for many intelligent and sensitive beings the world of the mid-20th century has lost its meaning and simply ceased to make sense. Previously-held certainties have dissolved, the firmest foundation for hope and optimism has collapsed. Suddenly man sees himself faced with a universe that is both frightening and illogical — in a word, absurd." (1)

That the world is illogical and life itself is absurd, seems the fearful conclusion of modern thought. The artist, because of his sensitivity, must feel this more than most. The Aristotelian universe of fixed stars with the planets describing a perfect circle has gone. The Christian view of a universe created and upheld by God has disappeared from modern thinking. Darwin's theory, transformed into a myth, of man rising from the primordial slime to conquer the universe now, in the self-destructive orgy of the 20th century, seems old fashioned romanticism. Man is alone in a meaningless universe but the age-old questions remain fixed in the heart of man. There remains the eternal 'Why?' even when there is no hope of an answer.

In this situation the genuine artist is faced with a choice. He can protest against or accept the absurdity of existence; he can reveal the disorder or seek to impose order. Whatever choice he makes he is asserting, not simply his craftsmanship, but his essential humanity. Man is free to choose and impose.

So the protest, and even acceptance can be a form of protest, can be seen in much modern art. It is a deeply-felt protest against the machine that contemporary life is reduced to, the loneliness of modern man, and the despair that lurks in the human heart.

The Machine

It is not simply that man now finds himself living in a meaningless universe, but that it seems to be an increasingly hostile one. Ironically, much of this feeling of being pressurised into a non-human mould is the result of technological advances in every area of life. In a technical age, where the powers of the machine seem unlimited, it is man himself who seems threatened. The individual is weak, poor and hopelessly inefficient compared to the abilities of the machine.

But it is not simply the machine as a mechanical artefact which creates the danger but the growth of a technically-oriented Society as communities, nations, industry and leisure are all organised to be technically efficient and are bureaucratically structured. The individual ceases to be important in such a structure and is merged into the faceless man of the masses.

So it is not surprising that the artist finds himself threatened and in conflict with the machine. As a sensitive individual he must find himself opposed to the mechanistic view of life and the bureaucratic structures that dominate Western civilisation. In previous generations there was the myth of the 'noble savage' and men like Gauguin who turned their backs on civilisation and searched for a dream in the South Seas; or the myth of the 'garret' where a poet or writer could escape the demands of the organised life.

Today there is an easier and more accessible way. Rationality is the hallmark of the machine and irrationality seems the only way out.

As Jacques Ellul has written in his study of the modern world: "A major section of modern art and poetry unconsciously guides us in the direction of madness, and indeed for modern man there is no other way. Only madness is inaccessible to the machine." (2)

The machine may indeed write a better sonnet than a man; may indeed be able to produce better symphonies, plays, poems, novels and pictures, but the machine is predictable. It is mechanical and logical so one way for a man to assert his humanity is by being unpredictable and illogical. Madness is inaccessible to the machine. A machine will never stand on its head and create a poem which is meant to be recited backwards – but a man can do that and that man is often the modern artist.

This is one of the main reasons that there is so much of the irrational in contemporary art. Probably the ultimate in human irrationality is for the artist to try and turn himself into a machine; yet this is what some artists have tried to do.

The Pop Artist, Andy Warhol, has said: "The reason I'm painting this way is that I want to be a machine. I think it would be terrific if everyone was alike." (3)

He carried his views to their logical conclusion by calling his studio 'the factory' and applied the principles of the assembly line to produce what he called 'consumer art'. By using a photographic image and a silk-screen process he was able to turn out a large number of canvases and, to make the work quicker, he could employ a large number of assistants on the 'assembly line'. In Warhol's earlier films there is the same mechanical, almost non-human, approach to his art. He made a number of films and his technique was simple; he would set up a camera and let it run for hours. *Sleep* was a six-hour film of a man sleeping; *Kiss* was a film of a kiss slowed down so that it lasted for eight hours, and *Eat* was a marathon six-hour film of a man eating. Perhaps it is not surprising that Andy Warhol is on record as saying that he liked boring things!

Another way for an artist to turn himself into a machine is by seeking to produce art without any conscious control of the medium — art without craftsmanship. So paint has been fired from a shotgun onto a canvas and even an artist's palette has been exhibited as an artistic painting. In music and poetry attempts have been made to remove human rationality in the name of art. There is music produced by random selection; John Cage composed by tossing coins to decide what notes to use and then using the ancient Chinese book, *I Ching*, a work that was intended to give forecasts according to the throwing of coloured sticks. Poetry has been written according to the sounds of the words rather than the meaning, or even by picking names or phrases from a telephone directory or newspaper. All this ensured that whatever was created was not the conscious effort of skill, craft or rational ability.

In theatre this was reflected by the movement known as the Theatre of the Absurd. Rationality was turned on its head, plots were worked out logically upon an illogical basis and characters lived within an irrational world. While the Theatre of the Absurd movement appears to have abated, the influence carries on in the presentation of drama.

All these have been a deep-rooted protest at the condition of man in a world that has simply ceased to make sense. The most influential philosophy behind it all has been existentialism. This is the conviction that rationalism has failed to find objective truth, objective reality and the meaning or essence of man; all we can know is our existential experience at the existing moment. Existentialism has had a far-reaching effect on the contemporary arts and its basic irrationality has been used as a vehicle of a profound protest. In the post-war years in Europe there have been two main streams of protest; Marxism in the streets and existentialism in the theatre and the arts.

Interestingly, and for the Christian significantly, man remains man in spite of the theories of the philosophers and images of the artists. As a creature, made in the image of God, morally responsible and rational, he cannot deny his character and humanity. So it is a fact that all attempts to show the absurdity of life in the arts does, contrarily, reveal something of the essential dignity of humanity. The images may be destructive, the portraits distorted, the resemblance to reality deliberately corrupted, but true reality keeps breaking in. Whatever may be said or done, man remains a creature who is God's image-bearer.

Samuel Becket's play *Waiting for Godot*, the forerunner of the Theatre of the Absurd, presents two men waiting in some strange no-man's land. It is a play of intense pessimism, nothing happens and the audience know nothing is going to happen; they wait for Godot and Godot is not going to come. The two characters, cosmic tramps, while away the time word-spinning and assuring one another that, if Godot comes then, as one says, "We'll be saved". The characters seem worthless, irrational, yet they retain a great measure of human dignity. They are human beings. This is true of all Becket's plays; characters may live in dustbins, be buried to their neck in rubbish, they may have no past and no future, their talk may be obscure and irrational, yet in spite of all they remain creatures of humanity, so that we can identify with them and share their suffering and experience.

Another dramatist, Eugene Ionesco, has written a number of plays where the characters find themselves in bizarre and grotesque situations. They struggle with a corpse which grows several feet a day, or wrestle with such arithmetical problems as 'four minus three', yet they retain the dignity of human beings. Whatever context men and women are artistically presented in, something of the nobility of human life cannot be totally destroyed.

The same is true in the effect of the non-verbal arts. The multifaced characters of Picasso and the distorted portraits of Francis Bacon affect us because we know that they represent human beings. It may be a corrupted reality with the facial features melting away or brutally fragmented, but the features shock us because we know the true reality of a human face and recognise what is being done to humanity. In Avant Garde music, the discords and obscure cacophony of sounds offend because our ears insist in trying to impose pattern and harmony. Where dignity and purpose are destroyed the human mind is so made that it cannot truly function and will insist on trying to impose form and meaning.

In all the contemporary arts there can be seen a protest against the destruction of humanity and the images, symbols and myths disclose the full horror of individual life in a mechanised world and a closed universe. This vision is further outraged by the isolation and terrifying loneliness that marks modern man where God seems to have departed from the heavens and there is no community.

The Loneliness

It is not surprising that, in the late 20th century where the loneliness of the city is infinitely worse than that experienced by Robinson Crusoe on his desert island, the arts protray and protest at the isolation of the individual. 'It is not good that man should be alone' is the Word of God but today man is increasingly alone. God has departed from the culture and thought–life of man and there is only a barren universe above, a mechanised society around, and everything encased in a meaningless determinism.

There is much loneliness and alienation reflected in modern art. Paintings do not only portray the disintegration of individuality, but the painful isolation of people one from another. Francis Bacon paints portraits of modern man as a being who is losing his identity and melting away into nothing. In his 'Figure in a Landscape' there is a man sitting on a chair, but there is a terrifying blackness in the place where his head should be. In his series of paintings reinterpreting Velazques's 'Portrait of the Pope', Bacon reduces the bust of the Pope to an image of despair. He becomes almost a headless figure, imprisoned in a transparent box, screaming in the agony of desperation. The Official Guide to the Tate Gallery says of Bacon: "The theme which occupies him repeatedly is the isolation of the individual human being who is usually depicted seated in a claustrophobic windowless interior." (4)

The sculptures of the contemporary Alberto Giacometti also reflect this loneliness in an interesting way. Much of his work consists in making long, elongated figures, or groups of figures, built on a wire foundation. These figures are always alone. Even when they are in a group they are all facing different directions or walking away from one another. There is no communication between them, no personal relationship, only loneliness and isolation.

Music can be a powerful medium for expressing the intense loneliness that lies in the heart of 20th-century man. It may be the meaningless clamour of the avant garde or the wail of the pop song, but it carries a wistful – or painful – longing for love and community where life can have a place. A wondering 'where all the lonely people come from'.

Certainly novels and poems often explore the theme of loneliness, and drama is frequently concerned with the isolation and aloneness of characters who are incapable of communicating with one another. Arthur Miller's play, *Death of a Salesman* shows a salesman who, in his own words, 'fails to lick the system'. He is the modern man of the affluent society, conditioned to the idea of success being a good job, a good bankbook, and a life which is made rich by influential friends and admiring neighbours. But the pressures of his job, and the pressures of his society, distort and corrupt all that is worthwhile in human relationships. He ends up conscious of his failure in every sphere of life and the only way out lies in suicide. At the heart of it all, in spite of the apparent gregariousness of his nature and community, he is a very lonely man.

The pain of loneliness can be assuaged by death and this is the dilemma; is death the only cure for a meaningless life? The search for the answer to that question was one of the main preoccupations of Albert Camus. He saw modern man as finding himself in an unintelligible universe and having to learn to live without hope or absolute knowledge, yet having also to reject the path of suicide and despair. So in his book, *Sisyphus*, Camus takes as his hero the character in Greek mythology who had to spend eternity rolling a huge boulder up a hill only to find it rolling back down again, and having then to start afresh his senseless task. Sisyphus is modern man, seeking to find meaning, satisfaction and contentment in a futile struggle. It is not surprising that it is almost impossible to escape the agony of despair.

The Despair

In the arts, as in all of life, it is but a small step from protest to despair. So in many of the contemporary arts there is a strong undercurrent of despair. It is difficult to walk through a modern art gallery and come out with a light step and happy heart.

The problem is that no matter where the artist turns to find real solutions to real problems, there is no answer. Beauty, joy and humanity seem out of place in a technically-organised society. In a one-dimensional world there are no stars to soar beyond or horizons to cross; materialism has no place for the things of the spirit. Yet the search must go on. The struggle to find and reveal the lost glory of man and creation must continue even when there is the fear that there is no answer.

Ionesco dramatised this brilliantly in his play, *The Chairs*. An old lighthouse keeper facing death has decided to invite many and important guests to hear his words of wisdom. Perhaps the answer to the riddle of life will be given. So, frantically, he and his wife struggle to seat the imaginary people who come – perhaps a symbol of modern man striving to create order out of chaos and meaning out of nothingness. The final, bitter irony is that the old man can neither read nor write and the curtain falls to the sounds of what appears to be the moans and groans of a deaf mute trying to communicate. Perhaps the answer is that there is no answer.

It is not just that there are no answers; somehow there no longer seems to be a real world 'out there'. Objectivity has given way to subjectivity. The founders of modern art did not believe they could captive the real world, all they could hope to do was give an impression, but even this failed. All movements in modern art, beginning with the Impressionists, have ended, via distortion, in abstract patterns. They have ended as dreams trying to communicate to dreams. Art has been driven in on itself with private visions being presented for private interpretation. But a retreat from rationality and reality can only lead to despair.

Of course there is still much art which ignores the basic dilemma of 20th-century man. There is still escapist literature, sweet romantic tunes, amusing and entertaining plays, pleasant films and eye-catching, naturalistic paintings which are easily understood and appreciated. Nevertheless the main stream of the arts have been in the general direction of a deep protest mingled with an underlying despair. The serious artists of this century have faced the ultimate horror in the departure of God and man in an inexplicable universe.

Some now see art as losing its meaning and purpose. As one contemporary artist has asserted: "Man now realises that he is an accident, that he is a completely futile being, that he has to play the game without reason . . . all art has become a game by which man distracts himself." (5)

Can there be anything more despairing that for art to become a game – a mere amusement? The arts, a gift of God for the delight of men's hearts, to stimulate mind and imagination, to enrich life and experience and enlarge vision and perception – all reduced to entertainment. A distraction from a meaningless life.

But whatever the artist may do, whatever conclusions he may reach, the questions remain.

> "Where is the life we have lost in living?
> Where is the wisdom we have lost in knowledge?
> Where is the knowledge we have lost in information?
> The cycles of heaven in twenty centuries
> Bring us farther from God and nearer the dust." (6)

6

THE HOPE OF MYSTICISM

If the agony of protest fails to unite all the dimensions of life – physical, spiritual, emotional and rational – where do the arts go? They cannot remain static or they will fossilise into an empty tradition. To retreat into mere entertainment or distraction is to deny their calling. The arts must develop, experiment and expand into a living culture or they will become the memories of a past age. Apart from suicide the only answer to despair must lie in the direction of hope and it is towards this that the arts of the late 20th century are moving. They are seeking a new mysticism.

Hope and faith would seem to be the answer, giving a new mysticism where the irrational present may be seen as the dawn of a more rational future, and the meaninglessness of contemporary existence is the herald of a deeper meaning and purpose. It is hope without substance and faith without knowledge. It is mysticism with a difference.

The early Mystics believed there was a God who communicated with men and that there was a spiritual dimension to the physical world. As their works show, this communication may be obscure, even apparently irrational, but it was a real message from a real God. The spiritual dimension was not an extension of the physical, or mental plane, but a reality, perhaps more real than the physical.

Today much modern art is seeking to present a mysticism with nothing there. It is taken as self-evident that there is no God such as Christians have believed in for centuries; the biblical God, Creator, Sustainer, Sovereign, Righteous, Holy and Loving, is taken as a myth. But this has not halted the search for a spiritual reality, indeed today the search is more intense. The arts are seeking to find and reveal something 'other', some deeper or higher reality – a mysticism with nothing there. In seeking to transcend the closed universe of the contemporary world view they, by denying God and His revelation, do not know where it can be found. So they turn to a mysticism in sex, in religion, or on mysticism itself.

In Sex

The struggle to find a transcendant reality is one of the reasons why there is so much sex in modern art. In a world without meaning, the primal urge, according to some modern psychology, may create meaning and purpose. It is felt that in sex true humanity can be asserted and man can rise above the mechanistic life he has inherited. Sex also is inaccessible to the machine. Sex is the gateway to a spiritual reality and consummation.

In the Longford Report on Pornography, Peregrine Worsthorne wrote: "But we do not live in an age of faith. Most of us do not know God and must perforce rely on human love for inspiration and solace, and such intimations of immortality as we experience come through its wonders and mysteries. This is why sex is so crucial to modern man. It is the force which can carry him upward to the highest pinnacles of human love. The artist may have other ways of perceiving truth and beauty. But to the ordinary mortal, cut off from God, love of man for woman, consummated in the sexual act, is the only remaining pathway to that state of holy bliss which earlier generations found through divine worship." (1)

Sex has become almost a mystical reality, not simply expressing the deepest meaning of humanity, but offering the 'pathway to that state of holy bliss' which transcends the physical world. So in many modern paintings, where the human figure is distorted and fragmented, sex remains; there are breasts and phallic symbols. Whatever else is destroyed sex remains recognisable – it is all that remains to prove the essential humanity of man.

In many plays and novels the only real contact people have with one another is often the sexual link; it may be all they have in common and all that they can understand. The sexuality of their words and actions may be the totality of their humanity. This trend has meant that much modern literature reduces all problems to sexual conflicts and all answers are to be found in making a successful sexual relationship. This examination, and exploration, of sexuality has become more and more explicit, moving from heterosexual relationships into homosexuality, lesbianism, promiscuity and every possible variation. Many of these plays and novels are only possible in the current decline of moral standards – a decline which the arts have helped to create.

But sex, and sexuality, are valid subjects for an artist to explore. The tragedy is that the exploration has tended to become exploitation and exposure has become over-exposure leading to self-destruction. Sex has become a trivial titivation to attract and shock leading to cheap art that shows no craft. The arts can, and should, enrich life and illumine the human condition, not pander to the desires of the mob. At times it appears that the battle for artistic freedom of expression has been won for the benefit of the pornographic merchant and to the profit of those who see sex as a saleable commodity.

But the strong emphasis on sex in so much of the modern arts raises questions deeper than the surface morality involved in the arts, artists or society. It raises the basic question 'what is man?' By concentrating on sexuality the arts must end by making man less than man. It reduces humanity to less than rational beings and portrays them as animals.

Even the genuine artist, in his honest seeking, cannot make sex into the ultimate transcendental reality which alone gives meaning to life. Man is more than a copulating animal and to portray him as such is to add to the latent despair that lies in the heart of 20th century man. To extend sex to cover the totality of human aspirations and experience is to bind man in the chains of his physical behaviour and imprison him back in the physical world.

The mysticism of sex becomes destructive when sex is removed from love and the true context in which it was meant to function. Like the arts, it is a gift of God, given for His glory and our good. It is part of humanhood, but only part, and given to be used in the relationship of marriage. It should be a joyous celebration of love, not a sensationalism which can only lead to corruption of what it is to be truly human.

Sex cannot be the final, ultimate answer to the deepest problems and longings of the human heart. So the arts must find another sphere where they can disclose something of truth and value to a world suffocating in materialism. They turn to the age-old means by which men lifted their hearts and soared beyond the stars; they turn to the mysticism of religion and in particular, in our own culture, to Christianity. But it is still mysticism.

In Religion

As the arts operate through the imaginative use of myth, image and symbol, then the easiest, and most convenient, to use are those from the disappearing Christian culture. While in the arts, as in other spheres, there has been a growing interest in other world religions, in Western culture it is still Christianity that is the dominant heritage. Although diffuse and corrupted, there is still a residual Christianity in the mind of Western man. The new mysticism is being sought there.

A drama critic, some years ago, praised the dramatic ending of a play, telling how a defeated, lonely man stumps off the darkening stage and music swells up as the curtain falls and "Bach's buoyant certainties well up once more to send us, too, off with firm step". (2)

So modern man, defeated and lonely in the darkness of the 20th-century stage, jumps back into the Christian certainties of an 18th-century Christian even although he knows nothing of the God who made Bach's music so triumphant and certain.

It is here that the situation becomes confusing, and dangerous for Christians. Artists are using Christian symbols and language for their work and so it appears to be Christian Art. But these images and symbols are being presented by men who do not accept the Christian revelation and have no Christian world view. They are creating a new form of mysticism by taking the images of a past Christian culture and using them to transcend the existential present. They are simply using myths and symbols to assert a leap of faith into a world without reality. It is faith, not based on the Bible or the Living God, but simply on the need for 'something there.'

The religious art of Salvadore Dali illustrates this trend. His 'Last Supper' shows a ghost-like Christ superimposed upon a Christ sitting with his disciples at the last supper. It is this transparent Christ who dominates the picture; a mystical Christ who obviously does not belong to this physical world and is more ghost-like than real.

Dali's equally famous 'Christ of St John of the Cross' is another example where Christ is removed from the everyday world of men. The cross, with the dying Christ who has no blood on his hands, head or feet, is mysteriously suspended between heaven and earth. The heavens are black, shutting him off, while on earth men go about their daily business with no interest – or responsibility – for the man on the cross.

Jesus Christ, although the Son of God, was a real man in a real world. He knew what it was to be tired, hungry, thirsty and knew the reality of pain and death. He lived, bled and died in this world, but Dali has changed Him into a mystical figure who belongs to a mystical realm far removed from the reality of physical existence. To look at the Christ portrayed by Rembrandt is to see how different was his view of the Saviour of the world. Rembrandt showed the Lord as a man involved in the lives of ordinary people, part of the world of men.

The same mysticism is seen in the theatre with the rock musicals, *Jesus Christ, Superstar* and *Godspell*. It is also noticeable in plays and films depicting the life of Jesus Christ. What is really significant is that they all effectively end at the crucifixion. The resurrection is practically ignored. Certainly in the rock musicals it is often asserted that the resurrection is implied in the music, and in plays such as Dennis Potter's *Son of Man* the implication is that it is the message of Jesus that is eternal. The glossy Hollywood epics usually present a multicoloured screen, the music of violins or the 'Hallelujah Chorus', as the most suitable treatment for the resurrection. The Gospel records are treated as factual but when it comes to the resurrection there is a move towards portraying it as non-factual. It seems to me that this is symptomatic of a desire for a mysticism with nothing there.

Even a vague knowledge of the New Testament reveals that the early Church did not imply the resurrection – it proclaimed it. It treated it as fact. The resurrection was not a mystical event which could only be understood through poetry, music or religious imagery but, as Paul argued to the Corinthians, it was a brute historical fact which could be verified by eyewitnesses. Modern artists, retelling the story for our age, want to remove the resurrection to some mystical realm where all things are possible and nothing can be proved, verified or denied.

In all the arts there are still to be found the images and symbols of the Christian Faith. Poetry and drama often re-echoes the liturgy of the Church or the words of the Bible. The great Christian themes of guilt, repentance and salvation, or the longing for the lost Eden and hope for the coming Kingdom are sometimes reflected in the modern arts. But it is not enough to take them at their face value and assume that they are Christian. More often than not, the artists make no confession of the Faith and are simply seeking to use the age-old images to convey a new vision that, in the final analysis, is not based on the Christian revelation.

So some form of transcendancy is being sought in the contemporary arts by using any symbol or imagery to express the intuitional fears, hopes and existential fears of modern man. It is an attempt to escape the trap of the material – and materialistic – world. Mysticism may be another name for irrationality but the end result is the same if there is 'no one at home in the universe'.

In Irrationality

There has always been an element of mysticism in the arts; magic and mystery seem part of all real artistic work. After all, who knows what the smile on the Mona Lisa really means? Yet it was the skill of a craftsman that enabled Leonardo to make the smile mysterious, he used the sfumato technique by making the shades blend into one another without clear lines.

But in the 20th century meaning has been sought, not through rational actions, but through total irrationality – the mysticism of meaninglessness. So the old rules of reason, logic and rational skill were thrown overboard and attacked as being worthless. The Dadaists, a group of artists who were influential during and immediately after the First World War, produced poetry which consisted of meaningless words and collages of coloured paper cut up and shuffled together. They were a revolutionary, confessedly anti-art, and totally irrational group who, at one exhibition gave axes to the viewers, inviting them to smash the exhibits and, on another occasion, presented a lecture on art which was given by twenty-eight lecturers in unison.

Dadaism gave birth to Surrealism, another group who again were unashamedly irrational. Surrealism not only affected painting and sculpture, but in many ways transformed the theatre, cinema and literature. It was pursuit in search of reality and, as such, was a new version of the age old question; "What is truth?"

What really happened in the arts was that the attempt to find something — or someone — 'out there' gave way to the search for something 'in here.' The Impressionists, rather than revealing what was 'out there', had simply shown what was inside their own heads. This led the way for the search to continue inwards. So the Surrealists, obviously strongly influenced by the theories of Freud, plunged deep into the subconscious and unconscious.

André Breton, one of the founders of Surrealism, wanted a 'pure psychotic automatism' as the governing principle of art. That is, an art that would be free from all reason, morality and even aesthetic considerations. It was a plea to abolish reason and turn the unconscious loose to let the flow of random impulses and thoughts create new things. Automatic writing and graphic art were comparatively easy but there were difficulties in applying the theory to painting. Max Ernst and Salvadore Dali were among those who showed the way.

Ernst produced paintings which seemed to be the visual equivalent of automatic writing. He used precise yet bizzare images in strange surroundings, like captured dreams which are fragmented and meaningless, yet seem to carry their own logic. Salvadore Dali introduced his 'paranoic-critical method' which was the theory of the artist painting as a paranoid without being actually mentally deranged. Like a madman the artist creates his own reality. Indeed Dali once said that the only difference between him and a madman was that he was not mad!

The Surrealists, in painting, did present a world of a frightening intensity; strange, haunting and sometimes fearsomely beautiful. Reality was turned on its head and dreams and nightmares became the reality. They seemed obsessed with the macabre and the erotic. Often with great draughtsmanship they brought unexpected things together in a shocking and startling way; a skeleton and nude woman stand together; a snake slithers down an ordinary staircase; a naked woman lies in a busy railway station, and a man looks in a mirror and sees the back of his own head. Often the backgrounds are mysterious, dramatic or even apparently extra-terrestrial.

But it was all more than simply a new way to look at reality. It was a new mysticism to find ultimate answers. It was an attempt, in Breton's own words, to find a "vantage point from which life and death, the real and the imaginary, past and future, communicable and incommunicable, high and low, will no longer be perceived as contradictions". (3)

In spite of the hopes and dreams it did not provide the answer. It is still a rational world and the answer cannot lie in the mysticism of irrationality. As Camus said, "Breton wanted both love and revolution at the same time, but they are incompatible". (4)

Although Surrealism, as a movement, went into decline after the second World War there is a sense in which the arts have never been the same again. The unconscious has been liberated and its mysticism still holds an appeal. The exploration has continued particularly under the influence of the drug culture. So there followed the rise of the psychedelic art and culture; art which was concerned solely with sensory perception and the deliberate distorting of reality to give the suggestion of hallucinations. It was an attempt to have the vision of a drug trip without the physical side-effects of introducing chemicals, like L.S.D. or Mescalin, into the body. Op Art works in the same area.

It is all a search, a seeking through a new mysticism, for the ultimate reality, the truth. Man cannot live by bread alone and an irrational jump into mysticism seems the only way of escape from the materialistic, technological society. Art cannot function in a one-dimensional world, and man was made for greater things than mere physical possessions. Although made of the dust of the ground he can never be content with mere dust.

The dilemma of modern man is brilliantly explored by Peter Schaffer in his play, Equus. It is the story of Alan Strang, a young man who has blinded six horses and is brought to a psychiatrist for treatment. The first problem is to find out why he did the horrible deed. The psychiatrist uncovers something of Alan's home life, finding that his mother is very religious while his father is a self-confessed, self-educated athiest. The earliest memories of the boy are of being taken for a ride along a beach by a stranger, an enjoyable experience interrupted by his parents. But his parents never seem to be in agreement; mother had placed a picture of Christ on the way to Calvary in Alan's bedroom, but his father had angrily torn it down and replaced it with a picture of a horse. With his religious and erotic impulses confused, Alan comes to worship this image of his God – Equus.

Getting a part-time job as a stable boy, Alan took to riding naked through the night, finding his own ecstasy. One night a stable girl takes him to a sex film where, to his horror, Alan sees his father. Going back to the stables the girl tries, unsuccessfully, to seduce him. She leaves and he is overwhelmed with guilt at his treachery to Equus, his only true God. He implores forgiveness but the horses just stare at him and in sudden desparation, Alan stabs out the eyes of the horses in the stable.

The play has further depths in that the psychiatrist himself is aware that his own life is devoid of passion, meaning or magic. It ends with him confessing that he can cure Alan, but it would mean taking away his capacity for reverence and rapture, it would destroy his wonder and worship. Conformity can be a form of death.

The arts have a part to play to show man that he is more than an animal, more than a creature of the dust. Equally they must show that he is more than the impulses of an irrational unconscious. He is a creature made in the image of God, morally responsible and rationally made to explore and expose the creation in which he is placed. Cut off from God the arts must wither and die; they have nothing beyond to reveal and end with a mysticism with nothing there.

Ionesco, who is no Christian, has confessed: "Humanist culture has thrown us back on ourselves, which is exactly what we sought to avoid. It has all recoiled upon us. Our desires and our passions which we thought were suppressed returned unchained ten times, nay a thousand times, stronger. One can count on one hand the words created out of joy and contentment and destined to bring us joy and contentment." (5)

He goes on to lament that culture has become humanistic instead of metaphysical, more psychological than spiritual. He asserts that we have forgotten how to look up, how to listen to the music of Bach and Mozart. No longer can we understand the smiles carved on the saints and angels in our cathedrals. In spite of having lost the wonder and awe of Bach and Mozart, Ionesco ends: "I have been very pessimistic. We still have Mozart who speaks to us of another joy, as inexplicable as it is profound." (6)

It is an attempt to bring the arts of the past into the mysticism of today; but the answer does not lie in mysticism. Ionesco does not ask if Mozart found the joy 'inexplicable' or if Bach considered his triumphant music the result of a mystical experience without rational foundation. Modern musicians, like those in all the arts, have not only lost the vision of the artistic creators of past generations, but they have lost the base, the faith within which many of them worked. Whistling in the dark cannot bring light.

So the arts of today are indeed in confusion, protesting, despairing, being mystical yet they are reflecting and shaping the modern world. Is there still another way? Is there a Christian way? Christians may be called to condemn or praise but before this can be done there must be understanding. Then the very confusion of the arts may be the greatest challenge, and opportunity, to show the path of hope and fulfilment where the arts can enrich, ennoble and refresh life.

PART THREE

TOWARDS A CHRISTIAN CRITIQUE

7

COMMITTED ART?

If the contemporary arts are in a state of chaos, a shattered mirror reflecting a broken world, does the answer lie in a unifying philosophy? Should the arts be an expression of commitment? Indeed is 'committed art' art at all? Then, for the Christian, there is the basic question as to whether there is such a thing as 'Christian art' or is art just good or bad on artistic terms? These are all relevant questions.

Undoubtedly there has been art committed to a political philosophy. Russia has sought to establish a strictly proletarian art which reflects the sufferings, aims and aspirations of the workers. The art-form of social realism. Marxism, in its many branches, has long had an attraction for many artists; in the thirties a number of leading poets and writers joined the Communist Party, seeing their task as being the mouthpiece of the workers. Picasso was a member of the Communist Party, as was Hugh MacDiarmid and John Paul Sartre. Bertold Brecht was probably the most influential dramatist who used the theatre as a Marxist apologist, in order to work out, in dramatic terms, answers to contemporary social and political questions.

Today, in all the branches of the arts, there are artists committed to some political philosophy, usually left wing, and who see their art as commitment to that cause. But the question of the commitment of the artist producing committed art has been complicated by the dominance of politics. An artist, like any other man or woman, may be completely uninterested in politics, but political neutrality does not mean that he is not committed to something. Art can be many things but it cannot be neutral. It is always a positive assertion of something. Art cannot be 'for art's sake', it 'tells tales' about a man's heart and, for the Christian, it should be an expression of the faith once delivered to the saints.

Art for Art's Sake

Although it may be an old-fashioned argument, there are still those who think that the artist's only responsibility is to his art. They hold to *l'art pour l'art* – art for art's sake. They would see art as being separate from, and having no connection with, the everyday world of values and standards. So art must be judged on its own terms and the artist is called to express the beauty, reality and truthfulness of his own vision without any thought of its cultural or social implications.

It is argued that when an artist is committed to something other than his art then what he produces must be less than art and will degenerate into propaganda or advertising. The artist and his work belong solely to the aesthetic sphere and have nothing to do with commerce, politics, social or culture reality. Art is simply, and purely, art. It is not social concern, a political manifesto or a cultural proposal, for from the moment these come into consideration then the artist's vision becomes subject to some other authority than art. He is no longer governed by his artistic integrity alone.

The problem of 'art for art's sake' is that it is a fundamentally meaningless phrase. No human activity, in any sphere, can be seen as being isolated or existing solely for itself; all human actions must bring reactions and no man, or his actions, is an island. A true work of art is made to communicate, not to exist for itself.

As a human being the artist cannot claim to be exempt from legal, social or moral responsibilities of his actions and products. Many have claimed this privilege but the Christian view has not really been refuted – the greater the gift the greater the responsibility of using it for good. Artists are in the business of communication and, with imaginative skill and craftsmanship, they can communicate at a deep and influential level and help to shape and direct, no only individual lives, but cultures and nations.

Oscar Wilde's assertion that "There is no such thing as a moral or an immoral book. Books are well written, or badly written. That is all" (1) is a frightening statement. It implies that books advocating genocide, suicide, apartheid, racism or any other evil should be judged purely on literary style. Art is only for art's sake.

But art is never for its own sake. When an artist paints a picture, writes a book or a poem, produces a play, composes a piece of music or designs a building, he is making a statement, taking a position. He is not being neutral.

Truman Capote, the American author, wrote an account of a multiple murder, recounting the actual case of four members of a family who were murdered by two men on the 15th November 1959. This book, *In Cold Blood* was an attempt by Capote to write what he called 'non-fiction novel' of the murders and the police activity leading to the arrest, trial and execution of the murderers. It is completely 'neutral' book; there is no blame, no moral judgement, only the facts set down in a precise, unemotional way. Although factual it is not neutral. By refusing to take a moral stance or make any judgement, Capote is taking a position, a point of view in which to relate the events. As a writer he is entitled to do this, indeed it is necessary, but his book cannot be completely neutral. Facts not only have to be selected, they have to be interpreted. Selection and interpretation must be based on some position and some commitment.

As Herbert Read, the authority on art, has written: "we must recognise that in its plainest manifestations art always embodies some interpretation of life, whether poetic, religious or philosophical." (2) It is obvious that any interpretation must be made from some stance, from some philosophical position. Neutrality is a myth and 'art for art's sake' an impossiblity.

Art as Commitment

Men are so made that they must be committed to something. At heart man is a religious being whose religious structure demands that he must commit himself to something or someone. Man cannot find meaning within himself but must worship something other than himself. In this way the debate on the neutrality of the arts is irrelevant because commitment is part of being human. All men, and even the most gifted artists are no exception, are committed to something. This means that the artist's vision, expressed in his work, must come from his own higher commitment, his own religious or philosophical world view.

Using the word 'worship' in its meaning of the giving of worth rather than in a liturgical sense means that art can be worship. Indeed Calvin Seerveld, a Christian Professor of Aesthetics in Toronto, has argued: "Art is worship. Art is a symbolically significant expression of what lies in a man's heart, with what vision he views the world, how he adores whom. Art tells tales in whose service a man stands, because art itself is always a consecrated offering, a disconcerting yet terribly moving attempt to bring honour and glory to something." (3)

So the arts are more than items of interest or amusement – though they may entertain and bring the deepest of joys. They always show something of the artist's heart. The distorted, often repellent, figures of Picasso give something of his world view and vision of humanity. The paintings of the abstract school reveal their understanding of the world, and the shapes and designs of modern sculpture show their view of reality. In the verbal arts, the triviality of many modern novels, the confusion of the dramatist, and the fragmented lines and broken images of the contemporary poet all 'tell tales' of where they stand.

Whatever work of art a man produces, in whatever medium, he is expressing something of his commitment. He may be a Christian, a Humanist, an Existentialist, or a Marxist, whatever he creates will be coloured by and charged with his commitment. All men are affected by their beliefs – even the Nihilist positively believes there is nothing to believe in!

So the novels of D. H. Lawrence not only reveal his skill at recreating nature, evoking places and his mastery of vivid characterisation with deep psychological insight, but they tell a great deal about Lawrence. They disclose his attitude to sex, primitive emotions, human relations and his view of the rational faculty of man. They reveal his basic philosophy. Contemporary poetry not only shows a new approach to poetic language and the creation of fresh images but reveals facets of varying philosophies and world views – how the poets 'adore whom'. Dylan Thomas wrote lyrical poetry with surrealist images which captivate and intrigue, but they also disclose his personal religion in the celebration of human life, its procreation, growth and death against which we must rage. The essential nihilism which is at the heart of Picasso's philosophy can be seen in his many viewpoints, his changing styles and approaches. All the arts reveal aspects of their creator's commitment because a man's faith is worked out in his life and his beliefs are revealed in his works.

This means that this belief dictates the shape of the work and how it is developed. In his novel, *The Plague*, Albert Camus examinates how men react to disaster, although at a deeper level he is concerned with life in an absurd world. Dr Rieux, the principal character, simply does what he can for those who suffer, even although he can find no meaning in what is happening. If Camus had, in this novel, made the Doctor have a conversion experience after which he accepted that, behind and beyond all things, there is a God of love and justice in control, then Camus would not have been true to his own philosophy. Picasso would have contradicted his own commitment if, in his painting 'Guernica' he had superimposed Christian symbols to show that, in spite of sin and hate, divine redemption were still possible. If Godot had come in *Waiting for Godot* to rescue and redeem the two men then Becket would not have been consistent to his own world view or philosophical position. T. S. Eliot, because of his Christian commitment, could not deny the possiblity of redemption to the characters in his plays.

Of course it is true that no man can reveal his whole theology or philosophy in any single work of art, but each of his artistic offerings will show some facets of his faith and some aspect of his commitment. What a man believes must govern his work and cannot be separated from what he does or makes.

Commitment does not mean that the artist can only produce propaganda for his viewpoint. The arts should challenge, compel to think, create intense emotions and reactions, but they must always respect true humanity. The techniques of brainwashing are not an art form. The arts must seek to express the truth of the artist's vision and then leave the viewer, reader or listener to make up his own mind. The artist must let his art speak for itself.

The artist, in expressing his basic philosophy, may well find that he is speaking for more than himself. As a child of his age he is putting into concrete terms more than his own private view. Because of his sensitivity, gifted intuition and artistic craftsmanship, he can reveal the hidden longings and fears of his age. This is one of the reasons that the modern arts are so confusing and disturbing.

With the decline of the Christian world view and the collapse of the Christian culture with no unifying philosophy to take its place, the arts are showing the fragmented world we have inherited. Order, harmony and beauty no longer apply to life and they must be destroyed before new gods can be found to serve the new age. So the modern dramatist is showing, among other things, that there is no neat beginning, middle or end to life, that it is without shape or direction. Abstract painters are proclaiming that there is no unifying pattern, order or objective meaning in the universe. The lack of harmony and melody in much contemporary music and poetry are reflecting a world where these things have departed. So the artist can show, not only his own commitment, but the underlying philosophy of the age, the commitment of his culture.

The arts can be a confession of faith for an age. The poet can be the voice of the people; the musician can express new songs for the heart; the dramatist can explore the fears and desires hidden in human behaviour, and the painter can create the images that reflect the underlying reality of the age.

Art is not neutral, but an expression of commitment, a statement of belief. Must there not then be such a thing as Christian art?

Art as Christian

The most widely accepted method of judging whether any work is 'Christian art' is on the content of the subject matter. If the subject is biblical or Christian then the work is seen as Christian art. Unfortunately such a simple thesis can only lead to confusion.

Some of the most glorious of crucifixion scenes have been painted by artists with no Christian faith and the glossy Hollywood epics based on Bible stories were made for commercial rather than religious reasons. Many novelists and dramatists have taken stories from the Old and New Testaments and used them imaginately and creatively to end by saying something that is not Christian. As we have seen, artists today are using religious and biblical imagery which reveals a very doubtful Christian view. Subject matter is not enough to judge whether a work is 'Christian art.'

Rembrandt painted a number of biblical scenes and these are accepted as 'Christian art'; but he also painted many portraits, and a side of beef hanging in a butcher's shop. Milton wrote on classical themes, introducing Greek mythology as well as on the great biblical themes of creation, fall and redemption. William Cowper produced some of the finest hymns in the English language, yet also gave us 'secular' lyrics and humourous narrative poems. In this century Eliot has written such Christian poetry as *The Journey of the Magi* and even comic verse in *Old Possum's Book of Practical Cats*. It would appear that Christian artists have never felt bound to work strictly on biblical or religious themes.

What then is Christian art? There are those who would assert that the phrase is meaningless; that there can be no such thing as 'Christian art'. They see art as being only good or bad, true to life and reality or false to both. Art is simply a language, a means of expression, and can be neither 'Christian' or 'non-Christian'.

It seems to me to be philosophically, and theologically, necessary to argue that there must be such a thing as 'Christian art'. Undoubtedly there is unchristian art, even anti-Christian art. There is an art which denies the Creator and presents the creature to be worshipped. There are artists who seek to show that life is essentially absurd, who portray the universe as silent and meaningless, who hold that chance, man, or some other idol rules over all things. There is an art that implies that irrationality, sex, human experience or perception is the only reality. Such art is unchristian, indeed in the final analysis, it is anti-christian. Such art is the product of humanistic world views, expressions of a false philosophy and revealing an unchristian commitment in the artistic statements.

If there is unchristian and anti-Christian art then logical necessity forces the conclusion that there must be a specifically 'Christian' art. But Christian art is not Church-centred art. The arts are a gift of God, not given to the Christian Church, but a creational gift given to all mankind. They are there for the Christian and the non-christian, part of creation, part of our humanity. So the Christian can take them and bring them under the rule of Christ; as He is Lord of all then the arts can be used to explore and disclose all spheres of His domain.

So Christian art is not limited to religious subjects but to all of created reality. It is an art which is worked out from an artistically gifted, sensitively aware and sanctified imagination. It is the artistic expression of a Christian world view and philosophy which is rooted in God's revelation. As Rookmaaker summed it up: "In brief, the Christian character of a work of art consists in a healthy outlook on reality and human life, an outlook which has been nourished by Holy Scripture." (4)

Just as a truly Christian heart cannot help praising God so a truly Christian artist should not be able to produce anything but Christian art. The art should be the natural result of his faith. As Georges Rouault, the Christian painter saw it, there was no such thing as sacred art, only 'an art made by artists who have faith'.

But Christians should not only be interested in Christian art. All art has something to teach. Because the arts are a creational gift and God has, in His common grace, bestowed gifts to all men, they are for the good of all – even Christians. Indeed in the artistic and literary realms it appears that these gifts have been given more liberally to those who deny God. Calvin himself recognised this when he wrote: "These radiations of Divine Light shone more brilliantly among unbelieving people than among God's saints." (5)

Elements of the truth often appear in humanistic art and this should be no surprise. If the Christian view is true to reality then those artists exploring reality must reveal some facets of the truth. The pagan poet can open our eyes to the wonder and glory of creation, as can the painter, focusing our eyes on the branch of a tree or the textured beauty of an apple. The dramatist or novelist can, in their sensitive and penetrating studies, show something of the bewildered soul of modern man lost in a technological wilderness with no promise of a better land. So the themes of guilt, sex, alienation, loneliness, meaninglessness and death which occupy such a large proportion of the contemporary arts are expressing a true view of the human condition.

Samuel Becket, the influential dramatist and writer is not a Christian, but a Christian scholar has advised: "If you wish to meet, at a level of deep compassion and tenderness, with the soul of modern man, face to face with all the baffling paraphernalia of contemporary civilisation, turn to Becket's novels and to his plays. Nowhere more poignantly yet humourously are we searched out and known. Here, on a knife-edge between laughter and tears, one lives through an aching yet farcical bewilderment which lacks even the clarity of doubt, the rudder of defined uncertainty." (6)

The Christian can have no narrow world view or outlook. In Christ all things are his and he can appreciate all the gifts of God, even from those gifted who refuse to acknowledge the Giver. Of course, he must be aware that all that claims to be art is not necessarily art. In an age which has thrown off the supposed chains of tradition, anything new tends to be heralded as an artistic breakthrough and obscurity can easily be mistaken for originality. Those with little or no aesthetic appreciation can apply paint to canvas; those without rhyme or reason can write poetry, and some, with little knowledge of human nature can write plays and novels. It is an age when popular singers boast they cannot read a note of music.

The Christian will seek to understand and judge, not according to the fads and fashions of men, but in accordance with the Word of God. Even amid the encircling gloom of the 20th century the Bible can be a light to the arts and a guide to the path they should take.

8

SCRIPTURE AND THE ARTS

The Christian recognises that the Bible is God's word to mankind in written form. The purpose of the Scriptures is to lead us to salvation, to new life in Christ; this life, in God's providence, spills over into the life of the world, preserving and enriching it. But the Bible also teaches that the world's life itself is a gift of God, created and sustained by Him. So the Scriptures have much to say about the place and purpose of the gifts God has given in His creation.

The Scriptures assert that God alone is the Creator. He made the heavens and the earth and saw that it was 'very good'. Man was made of the dust of the earth; this means that he is made of the same material as the universe, his physical being consisting of the same elements as the earth so that he is not alien in the world. But he was made more than a physical animal at home in a physical world because God said, 'Let us make man in our image' and forming man breathed into his nostrils the 'breath of life'. Man is the image-bearer of God.

An image cannot exist on its own; it must have a reality behind it. So man was not made to be an autonomous creature capable of living in complete isolation from his Creator but, as Paul was later to argue, 'In him we live and move and have our being'.

Man was made to have dominion over all the earth — God's viceroy or steward in creation — and was given all the necessary gifts and capabilities to fulfil this task. But sin entered, man fell and with him all creation came under the judgement and curse of God. As Milton put it —

> Forth reaching to the fruit, she pluck'd, she eat:
> Earth felt the wound, and Nature from her seat
> Sighing through all her works she gave sign of woe
> That all was lost. (†)

All was lost. Instead of being at home in the world man found himself a stranger; he had been Lord of creation and now, through sin, the whole of creation fell with him. Sin meant he was separate from a holy God. He was alienated from the cultural mandate so that the task of caring for creation became a burden and a curse. He was even psychologically divided from himself because his desire to be completely free and autonomous conflicted with his God-dependent nature. Even his personal relationship with others was shattered. In every area of life, sin meant judgement and misery.

God did not destroy the world but through his Providence limited the power of sin, and still gives gifts to men. But, because of the Fall, man's basic reference point became himself and not the God he was made to serve. The gifts would be used to glorify man, the creature, rather than the Creator.

As is clear from the early chapters of Genesis, even with the cosmic effects of the Fall, man still had his God-given gifts and exercised them in many areas. He learned to make tents and become a nomad; Tubal-Cain learned to melt ores and forge instruments; Jubal exercised his skill in making pipe music and creating stringed instruments. All these abilities were creational possibilities inherent in the creation God has made.

The creativity and technical ability of man can be seen clearly in early history. It was so called 'primitive' man who first used the wheel, first melted iron, made glass, pottery, bronze, brass, knitting, weaving and developed cultivation. In all these things, even perhaps from wrong motives, he was obeying the original mandate to tend and cultivate the garden of creation and open up its riches.

Man was made to be creative and imaginative in every sphere of life and these things are not wrong; they are the gift of God. The Scriptures, while not a text-book on artwork or aesthetics, can teach us much on art and design; poetry and literature, and music, song and dance.

Art and Design

The first detailed account of artistic work in the Bible is in the instructions for the building of the Tabernacle in Exodus, chapter 25 ff. The instructions came from God and the design and artwork were all to be made according to His command. So, early in the history of the people of God, the arts were not forbidden but had a place in the corporate worship of His people.

The Tabernacle was basically a prefabricated building, capable of being dismantled and carried by the Israelites in their journeyings through the wilderness. Rather than a utilitarian structure serving a purely practical purpose, it had elements of artistic beauty, many items of real splendour and patterns and designs which would delight the eye.

While it was to be surrounded by curtains of goat's hair, hard-wearing and practical for a desert climate, the furnishings inside reveal aspects of creative art and craftsmanship. There were two altars, one overlaid with brass and the other with gold. The curtains surrounding the Holy of Holies were of fine linen, dyed in the bright colours of scarlet, purple, blue and white while the inner veil was embroidered with the figures of cherubims. The Ark of the Covenant was a chest of acacia wood, overlaid with beaten gold and covered with a lid of gold which was called the Mercy Seat. Attached to the Mercy Seat were two cherubims of solid gold, one on either side, spreading their wings as they faced one another and looked down at the Mercy Seat. There was a candlestick with a broad base and shaft of six branches, all beaten out of pure gold. The cups to hold the lamps on the candlestick were shaped like almonds while the base and branches were decorated with entwining flowers and leaves.

The details given of the Priest's robes show that they were colourfully made in gold, blue, purple and scarlet, and had jewelled engravings of the names of the Children of Israel. Around the hem of the robes were pomegranates of blue, purple and scarlet.

So in the Tabernacle many of the arts and crafts were brought together in the carvings, statues, embroidery and design. There was representational art in the carvings of leaves and branches and in the sculptured figures of the Cherubims; then there was non-representational art on the Priests robes with blue and purple pomegranates.

To a nomad people, living in the barren monotony of the desert, the Tabernacle would show another world of colour, harmony, proportion, beauty and brightness. It was God who gave these things because they were of value in the life of His people. So he took men and gave them the special gifts necessary to create the artistic decoration of the Tabernacle.

As we read (Exod. 31. 1ff), "The Lord said to Moses, 'See I have called by name Bezalel, the Son of Uri, Son of Hur, of the Tribe of Judah; and I have filled him with the Spirit of God, with ability and intelligence, with knowledge and all craftsmanship, to devise artistic designs, to work in gold, in silver and bronze, in cutting stones for setting, and in carving wood, for work in every craft. And behold I have appointed with him Oholiab, the Son of Ahisamach, of the Tribe of Dan; and I have given to all able men ability that they make all that I have commanded you." (R.S.V.)

It is interesting, and significant, that this is the first time in the Bible that there is mention of men 'being filled with the Spirit of God', and it was not for preaching or priestly activities but to have the ability to design, carve and create a building for the worship of God's people. They were given the gifts but, no doubt, they had to develop and work hard to bring the gifts up to their full potential. The gifts of God are freely given but they carry a measure of responsibility to men as to how they are to be developed and used.

Another interesting point is that the artists were not free to do what they liked but had to work within certain clearly defined limitations. They were given detailed instructions as to what was wanted and had to use their artistic skills in achieving that end in the best way possible. This has never proved a handicap to true art. Probably until our age, the artist has always had to work within certain restrictions or narrow conventions, but even within these limitations some of the greatest works of art have been created. Some of the finest paintings were created within narrow limits set by the patron; icons, murals and sculptures were made to suit the eccleciastical authorities; music was composed to fit special occasions or suit certain people, and even the strictest censorship did not kill the theatre or novel. True craftsmen and artists, like Bezalel and Oholiab, can work within tight parameters and still create works of joy, beauty and truth for the delight and illumination of all.

In the building of the Tabernacle the artist is not seen as a romantic lone figure working in isolation. There was a community of artists working for the community of people. It was a truly communal effort with the people bringing the gold, silver, bronze and other materials for the artists to use. True art is not produced in isolation and kept in isolation; it is for the community, for all men.

Albert Camus, an agnostic, recognised this fact when he wrote: "One of the temptations of the artist is to believe himself solitary, and in truth he hears this shouted at him with a certain base delight. But this is not true. He stands in the midst of all, neither higher or lower, with all who are working and struggling. His very vocation, in the face of oppression, is to open the prisons and gives voice to the sorrows and joys of all." (2)

The artists employed in the building of the Tabernacle were working and creating for the whole community, using their gifts in obedience to God. At a later stage in the Old Testament history the same principles were worked out in the building of the Temple. It was artists, exercising their divinely-bestowed gifts, working within God-given limits, creating something for the whole community with a view of bringing glory to God.

Art and design are not condemned in the Scriptures. It is not the making of images or representational art that is forbidden, but the 'bowing down to them'. It is idolatry that is condemned, not the production of artistic artefacts. The statues in the Tabernacle and Temple were acceptable, although the statue of the Golden Calf was condemned; but it was not the art of the sculptor that was evil – it was idolatry. The Golden Calf became an object of worship; rather than pointing to the Creator of all, it became an end in itself.

In spite of sin, the world is still a place of wonder and beauty. There are fruits and flowers, hills and valleys, seas and rivers, sunrise and sunset, and all, like the star studded heavens, declare the glory of God. The creativity of men is part of that glory. Given to fulfil the human life by adding fresh dimensions, challenging and entertaining, confronting and comforting. All these things the people would find when they entered the Tabernacle or Temple, lifting their eyes to the glory of the creation and helping the expression of their worship. '

Poetry and Drama

There is a considerable amount of poetry in the Bible. There are the poetic books such as Job, Psalms, Proverbs, Ecclesiastes and the Song of Solomon; apart from these, the Prophets often used the poetic form to convey their message and, in passages such as the prologue to the Sermon on the Mount, Jesus Himself used a poetic style.

Poetry, by the simplest definition, is a concise and skilfully arranged statement crystallising a thought, and as such has the greatest impact and is more easily remembered than a logically developed argument. So, apart from the pleasure and delight it can bring, it has a practical didactic purpose which the Prophets used. In poetic form their messages would be more easily remembered.

It is often assumed that poetry is the language of religion, the language of heaven. Certainly it has a sublimeness of thought and echoes of transcendancy which are the hallmarks of religion, and with its technical devices of metre, alliteration, rhythm and rhyme, can be seen as a form of incantation.

But it is to degrade poetry, and the Christian faith, to imply that poetry is the language of heaven. Christianity is intensely 'materialistic' – the Word became Flesh. Poetry can also be 'materialistic' – commenting on and illuminating all aspects of human life, physical as well as spiritual. It was Plato who held that the spirit was higher and more true than the physical; the Bible makes no such distinction. So the poetry of the Bible takes all the realms of creation for its provenance. The full range of human experience, love and laughter, tears and death, prayer and praise, and even sin and history are all expressed poetically within the pages of Scripture.

There is the celebration of love in the Song of Solomon. It is a poem, gloriously exotic and erotic, in praise of human love. In a joyous and lyrical way it celebrates the reality of human desire, sexuality and love and expresses the delight that a man and a woman can find in one another. There is rejoicing in each other's physical attributes and the way the body can create its sensations and emotions.

Of course, because it is inspired Scripture, God is speaking through the poem so that it becomes more than a love song and becomes a song of praise. It has deeper implications and a wider significance than purely as a love song, but this is part of the structure of poetry; the total becomes more than the sum of the parts and there are deeper and more valuable insights to be found beneath the surface interpretation.

But it is, along with its allegorical meaning, a song of love. So we have authority to assert that human, physical love, between bride and bridegroom, husband and wife, is not wrong and the celebration of each other is not sinful. A song of human love and the rejoicing in being truly human is pleasing and acceptable to God.

In the Psalms, the supreme poetry of the Bible, the same is true. They are not all concerned with mystical language and spiritual imagery; realistically down-to-earth they still remain poetry of the highest order. They are strong, emotionally moving and intensely human.

Many of the Psalms reflect the universality of poetry; they are personal but not individualistic. The Psalmist speaks for himself, expressing his own feelings and visions, but others can take his words and, recognising their truth in their own experience, make them their own. So the divinely inspired poet of Scripture can joyously affirm, 'The Lord is my Shepherd' and to others, far removed from the pastoral scene, the words remain true, personal and meaningful. The personal sorrow of Psalm 51 expresses the penitance of all 'whose sin is ever before me' and who, in humble helplessness, seek God's forgiveness. The rejoicing in the natural order of created things in Psalm 104, and the comforting recalling of history in Psalm 78, can crystallise the deepest emotions of joy and wonder of all those who have eyes to see and memories to recall.

The Psalms, like all the poetry of the Bible, are God-centred. Even where God is not mentioned by name, they are written within the context of the immanence of God. All of human life, physical and spiritual, mental and emotional, and all of creation are found to be suitably expressed in the poetic form. Rather than the language of heaven, poetry can be a means of seeing things on earth much clearer.

The Prophets also used a poetic form to express their message; Isaiah, Jeremiah, and most of the Minor Prophets employed poetry to deliver the Word of the Lord to their generation. But another art form which they practiced was dramatic technique. Often they would enact a situation or employ a dramatic presentation to add weight to their words. By acting, or going through a symbolic ritual, the Prophets aroused interest and captured attention.

It has been said that it is easier to write a book of philosophy than to produce a novel or a play. Certainly it is simpler to write about principles and imperatives than to deal with these things through real people in real situations. In drama, and the novel, abstract arguments are not presented but worked out in concrete situations. A philosophy and world view is made real, relevant and more easily appreciated.

What is significant is that God is the author of these dramatic presentations and they were undertaken by the Prophets on the express instructions of God. So, throughout the Prophetic books, there are many illustrations of the Men of God using drama, almost 'street theatre' to proclaim their message.

Jeremiah took the Elders and people to a valley outside the city and he carried a large earthen bottle; he then emptied the contents of the bottle on the ground before smashing it to pieces. He later repeated this action in the courtyard of the House of the Lord. This action was to show how God would punish their idolatry and sinfulness; it was a dramatic presentation of how the judgement of God would fall upon them. God would pour out the nation and smash it to pieces just as he had shattered the earthen bottle.

Ezekiel enacted out his prophecy of the scattering of the people of God. He cut his hair and divided the hairs into three lots; one third he burned in the fire, one third he tried to strike with the sword as he walked round the city, and the final third he scattered to the winds. From the hairs which he had scattered to the winds he kept a few and sewed them into the hem of his garment. All this was to show, in a dramatic way, what would happen to the people of God who persisted in ignoring the way of the Lord; they would be consumed by fire, perish by the sword and scattered to the four winds. Nevertheless, a remnant would be saved — just as he had saved a few hairs in the hem of his garment.

There are many such examples. Isaiah walked around Jerusalem barefoot, dressed in the garb of a slave. Jeremiah appeared in public with a wooden yoke around his neck to show how the people would be led away captive; when the Priests smashed this yoke he then wore an iron one that could not be broken. Ezekiel forecast the siege of Jerusalem by taking a large clay tablet and drew the outline of the city on it; then, using it as a backcloth, he built model siege works and trenches around it.

So as well as preaching the Prophets used drama. They knew it could be an ideal vehicle to show, in a personalised and realistic way, the truth that they proclaimed. Drama was a valid means of presenting God's Word, just as Jesus, in the New Testament, used dramatic stories in the form of parables to convey the truths necessary for an understanding of the will of God.

Music, Song and Dance

Other art forms described in biblical history include music, song and dance. Indeed music and singing occupy a great place in the life and worship of the people of God in the Old Testament and the Psalms, the hymnbook of Israel, is full of exhortations to the people to make music and 'sing to the Lord'.

Music is the finest means of expressing the deepest emotions. The whole range of human experience, from ecstatic joy to darkest sorrow, can be conveyed through music in a way that is not possible in verbal description or visual representation. It is an important part of human culture and its power to express pain or joy, happiness or grief, excitement or tenderness is recognised in the Scriptures.

The Children of Israel sang the Song of Moses after their escape from Egypt and the hordes of Pharoah. This song was an expression of the emotions and joy that was in their hearts; this song of deliverance will be completed in heaven when, according to John's vision, the ransomed people of God will sing the Song of Moses and the Lamb around the throne.

As we have seen, the Psalms are often songs of praise, and this singing of praise is carried into the New Testament where the Lord, after taking the last supper with his disciples, joined with them in singing a hymn before going out to Gethsemene and Calvary. Paul and Silas were able to sing hymns of praise in the dungeon of Philippi and the same Paul, writing to the Ephesians and Colossians, exhorts the Church to 'sing Psalms, hymns and spiritual songs with thanksgiving in your heart towards God'.

The Bible also shows music and singing related to sorrow. David composed a song on the death of Saul and Jonathan, an expression of mourning and pain at the loss of those whom he loved. Then there is the moving lament of Psalm 137 when

> By the waters of Babylon,
> There we sat down and wept,
> When we remembered Zion.

The torment of the captives was that they were expected to sing the songs of Zion in a strange land and their pain was too deep for words.

As with the other arts, music and song is acceptable to God when it is created within the context of a true relationship to Him. The singing around the Golden Calf was idolatry and condemned, but when it was the response of a God-centred faith then it was a valid and valuable activity for the people of God. This is not to say that all music should be 'religious' or performed purely in diets of worship.

As Calvin writes in his commentary on Genesis: "Because the invention of the harp and other musical instruments serves rather for pleasure and delight than necessity, it is not nevertheless to be considered altogether superfluous and still less does it deserve to be condemned." (3)

Music can delight and soothe the heart. David soothed the heart of Saul when he was disturbed and depressed and Elisha called for minstrels to play for him when the hand of the Lord was heavy upon him. Martin Luther, who shared Calvin's great love of music, recognised its worth. "Nothing on earth is more mighty to make the sad gay and the gay sad, to hearten the downcast, mellow the overweening, temper the exuberant, or mollify the vengeful." Then, with regard to choral works, Luther takes a delightful flight of fancy. "But when natural music is sharpened and polished by art, then one begins to see with amazement the great and perfect wisdom of God in His wonderful work of music, where one voice takes a simple part and around it sing three, four or five other voices, leaping, springing round about, marvellously gracing the simple part, like a square dance in heaven with friendly bows, embracings and hearty swinging of partners." (4)

We can almost see this happening in some of the Psalms where whole orchestras – and all the earth – is called to join together in singing praises to the God Who has done all things well. The same Psalms also exhort that the Lord should be praised in the dance.

Today the art of dancing has many connotations that make it difficult for many Christians to accept it as a valid activity, but the problem may be cultural rather than theological. In Western culture, apart from formalised art of Ballet, dancing has sensual and sexual undertones and has been associated with lasciviousness and immorality. Yet in the Bible there are many instances where dancing is recorded without condemnation.

David danced before the Lord, and although his wife rebuked him, it was acceptable to God. Another occasion, when David returned from a victory over the Philistines, the women came out of all the cities of Israel to dance and sing songs of Joy. The dancing of David and the women were basically the expressions of a deeply-felt joy that manifested itself in a dance. David was overwhelmed with happiness that the Ark of the Covenant was being brought back into his city and the women were jubilant at the victory over their enemies. Dancing seemed the natural thing to do. It is a natural response, the whole body being unable to contain its excitement at good news or triumphant events. Emotions can be expressed through bodily movement, whether spontaneous or formalised, and such a capacity is part of our humanhood and not inherently wrong.

But culture, and historical traditions, do affect attitudes to all the arts and in particular, dancing. Many Africans and West Indian Christians, who belong to an emotional and rhythmic culture, tend to sway or dance to the music of their hymns and it is a natural way of expressing their feelings and love of the Lord. Generally, in Northern cultures, where emotions are repressed, such behaviour appears to be unnatural and more rational actions are used to express emotions and faith. But the Bible teaches, in such passages as the dancing of David, that the art-form of dancing is not sinful in itself. It can be a valid response to the goodness of God.

Even the more stylistic forms of dancing, such as ballet or free expression, can be a valid means of non-verbal communication. Not only can it reveal the surging joy within the heart but can show the capabilities and potential of the human body to express a wide range of emotions through movement and actions. It is part of man's response in being a steward of creation, finding the possibilities and limits of the human body and experimenting with various means of expressing his deepest feelings and dreams.

In the Bible, dancing, like all the arts and all human activity, is judged in terms of its relationship to God. David danced and it was acceptable; the children of Israel danced before the Golden Calf and it was condemned – it was not the act of dancing that was condemned but the context in which it took place – idolatry.

The Bible shows that the arts have a place in human life. They are not used exclusively in services of worship but are part of the cultural and social life of a society. But they are judged in the context of an offering to God. The artwork of the Tabernacle and Temple; the poetry of the Psalms; the dramatic presentations of the Prophets, and the music, songs and dance of the people all rebounded to the glory of God. That is not to say that all the art was 'religious' in the commonly accepted meaning of that word; much of it was apparently 'secular'. Flowers, trees and branches were engraved in the furnishings of the Tabernacle and Temple; The Song of Solomon celebrates human love; many songs were exultant cries of battles won, and the Psalmist often rejoiced at the beauty of the earth. But all these things came from a God-centred view.

Therefore the biblical understanding of the arts has nothing to do with the medium used, or the subject matter explored, but is dependent upon the world view of the artist. God may not be explicitly mentioned, discussed or revealed in such art, but it will come from a heart which understands, and believes, that behind all created things there is a Creator who is the giver of every good and perfect gift.

The arts are a creational gift of God. All man's creativity — and science — are only possible through the Creator who made these things possible. Only a theology which begins with God as Creator can have a place for the arts. The Bible begins with God the Creator and has a positive place and role for the arts and crafts of mankind.

9

THE CHRISTIAN AND THE ARTS

If, as the Bible teaches, the arts are one of the good gifts of God, then the Christian has a responsibility, not only to value them, but to encourage their right use. They are acceptable to God and a necessary part of human life. A world without colour, music, form or patterns would be unthinkable, a denial of the glory and wonders of creation.

But the Bible does not give technical specifications on the form, structure or fashions of the arts. There are no detailed instructions given on how to write a poem, novel or play. No advice is given on how to paint a picture, or how to shape, carve and design a piece of sculpture. There is no practical teaching on how to compose music. The Bible does not offer tuition on the arts and crafts. What the Bible does give, apart from revealing the way of salvation, are the basic principles of behaviour and activity which should apply to all spheres of life. Working within these principles the Christian has the liberty of a child of God.

So the starting point for a Christian understanding, and contribution, to the arts must be a basic Christian theology because what we believe is never secondary to what we do. If we are vague, or uncertain, about what we basically believe then it will be impossible to work out a consistent Christian critique or make a positive contribution to the understanding or production of arts. What we believe, what lies in our heart, is worked out in our actions and the works of our hands. Faith is not, and cannot be, removed from action.

There is no need to develop a 'theology of the arts' – all that is required is a biblical theology that has a place for the arts. The Bible does give us this. All things were created to serve God and bring glory to His Name. But sin has corrupted all things and men are naturally in rebellion against God; they want to be 'as God', autonomous, going their own way, doing their own thing. This means a root contradiction in the heart of the natural man; he is totally dependent upon God for his very existence yet refuses to acknowledge that dependence. He uses the gifts of God yet does not know the Giver. But, through the grace of God in Christ, men can be brought back into a right relationship with their Creator and can serve Him as Lord and King. Salvation means health and freedom. No longer a slave to sin, the Christian is brought into a new freedom to appreciate, and use, the gifts of God. The arts are among those gifts.

Submission to God does not mean a narrow view of life or a curtailment of artistic or literary freedom. His Word is truth and the truth can make us free. It will open our eyes, not only to the plight, but to the possibilities of man. It will show that all things are ours — all subjects, all themes, and can be understood and explored by an enlightened mind and sanctified imagination.

So a biblical world view giving a God-centred approach to the arts does not mean a restricted vision or a making of the artist into a High Priest or Prophet. Neither does it mean that all art produced by non-Christians must be dismissed as worthless. What it does mean is that Christians can, and should, be involved in the arts; that all men have a measure of creativity and that art, even from those who deny or defy God can be of value to an understanding of the world in which we live and the truth that unites all things.

The Need for Involvement

'All art is quite useless,' (1) wrote Oscar Wilde. The arts do not function in the realm of materialistic practicalities, nor are they an activity which can be quantified by economic theory. They cannot be assessed purely in financial or material worth. So perhaps Oscar Wilde's verdict is not as glib or simplistic as it first appears.

Yet, tragically, many Christians would take the words at their face value and agree that the arts serve no useful function in the world. They would assume that all artistic activity is a waste of time and talent with artists engaged in what, at best, can only be described as doubtful activities.

Many Christians, particularly in the pietistic or evangelical tradition, have tended to be suspicious of the arts and to treat them as weapons of the Devil. So the theatre and cinema are considered 'worldly'; novels read for pleasure are suspect; paintings are acceptable if they are of religious subjects; music could be considered 'sacred' if it had Gospel words attached and, conversely, poetry would be permissible if it could be sung as a hymn or chorus. So the mainstream arts, and the vast body of artistic work have been ignored or attacked as belonging to the 'world' from which Christ came to save us.

But the 'world' from which Christ came to save us, and from which we are commanded to be separate, is the Kingdom of Darkness, the domain of Satan which is in rebellion against God. It is not the created order which God made and loves. The arts, no less than science, agriculture, understanding and wisdom, is a gift of God and part of His handiwork in creation. They exist because God thought it was good that we should have them in this life. Of course, Satan can use them, and men misuse them, but the arts are still a God-given gift. There is always the danger, as Calvin warned, that 'In despising the gift we insult the giver'. (2)

Unfortunately, the attempt to 'keep oneself unspotted from the world' by withdrawing from the sphere of the arts – and culture – has had tragic results. Among other things, it has reduced the Gospel to a matter of personal salvation and ignored the cosmic consequences of the Cross. The whole creation, cursed by the Fall, is awaiting salvation and will be brought under the Lordship of Christ in the coming Kingdom, the new creation. As part of that new creation, and already citizens of the Kingdom, Christians are called to work towards bringing all things under the Lordship of Christ until He comes to restore and renew all things. They are called to serve Him with the gifts He has given – and these gifts include imagination, intuition, craftsmanship and all the tools of artistic work. Jesus Christ is 'Lord of all' and there is no authority to say that His Lordship should not be exercised in the sphere of the arts.

Christians are meant to be salt in the world and a light to their generation. But retreating from involvement with the arts has meant an artistic culture developing without Christian salt to purify and preserve or Christian light to show the way. This means that much Christian criticism of the modern arts must be negative, condemning without contributing by being able to show a better way. As most of the serious contemporary arts are revealing a vision of despair, defeat, irrationality or a mysticism without foundation, the only truly positive and constructive criticism would be a Christian art that showed there is hope, meaning, purpose and the possibility of redemption in Christ. Only a Christian artist can work out, and show, what the Gospel would mean for the arts. But without salt the arts must become even more corrupt, and without light all artistic productions can only end by intensifying the darkness.

Withdrawing from the culture in a mistaken attempt to escape the 'world' has tended to make some Christians, not only anti-art but, even more serious, anti-intellectual. Not only do they fail to understand what the modern artist is trying to say or do, but they deliberately make no attempt to understand. This can only lead to a breakdown in communication and a failure to appreciate the forces and 'demons' let loose in our age.

The artists are the great communicators in human society, even in the age of the Mass Media. They are the music makers, the singers, the dreamers, the myth-creators and the thinkers. Not only do they hold a magnifying mirror to society, showing 'warts and all', they help to give it shape and direction. So if Christians turn their backs on the arts then they are in danger of being out of touch with modern man. Then they will be in the familiarly tragic situation of holding answers to questions no-one is asking and offering solutions to problems that appear to concern no one. The arts of our day, like all the disciplines of theoretical thought, are facing real questions and searching for valid answers. If the Christian will not listen, does not understand, then any contribution he tries to make will seem irrelevant, be apparently romantic rather than realistic.

Christians are called to serve God and be His witnesses in this world. They have to confront the world, not retreat into a cosy corner of pietistic conformity. In a world cursed by sin, where men exploit one another, where the arts can debase as well as ennoble, condemnation and censorship is not enough. It is not by repressive measures that the battle will be won. An alternative must be offered that shows sympathy, understanding and appreciation of the struggle to find direction, meaning and hope in the contemporary arts.

So Christians are called to proclaim, and live out the confession, that Christ alone is the way, the truth and the life, and that all authority, in heaven and earth, is given into His hands. The ability to create and make works of art are part of the world which God has made and no Christian can despise the good gifts of God. Creativity too must find the way, the truth and life and must be under some authority; anarchy and disorder cannot be art. Christians alone know the truth that "There is not one square inch of human life over which Christ does not say, 'I am King'". (3) This includes the world of the arts.

We are not all called to be artists and serve the Lord in the aesthetic sphere, but we cannot ignore a large part of the Kingdom of the King. It may be a rebellious realm, refusing to acknowledge the King, but it is still part of the Kingdom that will be brought under the rule of the Lord when all things are restored. Meanwhile, we are called to live out the Kingdom, point to its coming reality and witness to its power and authority.

Although all Christians are not highly gifted artistically, or called to serve within the sphere of the arts, they do have a responsibility to witness and be involved. In all the arts there is a need for Christian salt and light, not only by active participation, but by understanding, constructive criticism and real appreciation. The arts do not exist in a vacuum, but permeate all society. So there is a need for Christian encouragement to those, artistically gifted, who are seeking to develop and extend their gift. It was given for the glory of God and the good of the community of men. Christians who understand this should be in the vanguard, not mere spectators or hopeful followers of every new trend.

Above all there is the need of prayer. A need for Christians to pray to the Giver of every good gift to raise up men and women of artistic ability and integrity who will enrich and elevate the quality of life in the 20th century. There is much revealing the deep spiritual poverty of the age, there is now a need for those who had show the glory and splendour of a biblically-based, God-centred art.

We are not all artists, but we have all been given the gift of creativity.

All Are Creative

This is the age of mass production with standardisation as the hallmark. Cars, clothes, furniture and furnishings of all kinds roll off the production lines at an ever increasing speed and multi-national shops sell multi-nationally produced goods. The result is a world of concrete and plastic. Instead of each home being truly unique, a visible expression of the lifestyle and values of the family, they all become variations on a theme. The same nylon-based carpets, fibre-glass curtains, moulded ornaments, veneered furniture and the same glossy reproductions on the walls. Of course they are not all identical, there are variations in style and colouring, but only to the extent that the production techniques of mass production can allow.

The same is true outside the home. Economic pressures and the technique of mass production being applied to architecture has meant the destruction of much of the individual character of different areas within the country. There was a time when the patterns of buildings and architectural styles was distinctly different in every region and community. Houses and building were created by local men, using local stone and materials, and following local traditions. Now tower blocks and box-shaped bungalows of characterless design predominate throughout the whole country.

Cities were rebuilt and reshaped to suit the motor car and the technological world of communications and industry. The old landmarks were torn down, leaving people as strangers within their own community. It should not be surprising that human problems multiply and the individual feels threatened.

Families are not sociological units that can be fully satisfied with shelter and economic prosperity. Man is not a consumer to be manipulated or an extension of the machine. Men and women were created to live in community, relating, not only to one another but to all of creation. They need the stars. They need colour and beauty, harmony and fulfilment. They need to exercise their God-given creativity.

So the uniqueness of the individual cannot be obliterated by all the technical society with its emphasis on the economic efficiency of standardisation. People, sometimes almost despite themselves, still persist in being individuals, striving to express their personality, and resisting the ultimate in functionalism where every home is an exact replica of the next, every lifestyle in precise conformity with every other one, and a grey standardisation hangs over all.

Therefore in an age of mass production and standardised cheap products there has been a rapid growth of interest in 'do-It-yourself' and crafts and hobbies. But even here, in these objects of creativity and craftsmanship, the technical society takes over by producing plastic kits, clip-on models and painting by numbers. 'Art' that requires no ability beyond the simple reading of instructions and following comic strip directions. But the very existence of these items, serving a real need, shows the innate desire for human beings to be creative.

As we have seen, John Calvin, who according to the popular myth was not sympathetic to the arts, recognised that all men have a measure of artistic ability: "But although all are not equally able to learn all the arts we have sufficent evidence of a common capacity in the fact that there is scarcely an individual who does not display intelligence in some particular art. And this capacity extends not merely to the learning of the art, but to the devising of something new, or the improving of what has been previously learned." (4)

All men are not equally gifted but all men have a measure of the gift of creativity. All men have a degree of craftsmanship though most do not attain the heights we call 'art'.

But in our society, with the strong influence of the Enlightenment, the tradition has grown that the arts are essentially an élitist activity which has little relevance for the vast majority of people. This is a false view; the arts are for everyone, to enjoy, appreciate and be involved in. The artwork of the Tabernacle and Temple was for the aesthetic benefit of all and the Psalms, poetry, music, stories and drama in the Bible were not for a narrow élitist audience but for the enlightenment and enrichment of the whole community of God on earth.

It is a fact the plays of Shakespeare were not written as examination material for a course in English Literature and were not first performed for a middle-class intelligentsia. Bach did not write his music for 'high-brow' critics, but for an ordinary Church congregation. Ploughboys and maidservants parted with their wages and did without necessities to buy the collected poems of Robert Burns. In the 19th century the great novelists of Russia and England did not write their works as academic studies for a select readership. It has long been the tradition for even the poorest of families in Holland to spend money on original oil paintings and, in the pre-war depression, for the poor of Amsterdam to stand outside in the cold, listening with rapt attention, to musical concerts being given in the warmth of a Church or Concert Hall. All men can respond to the arts.

This response comes because all men have a measure of creativity and have been gifted with imagination and the ability to dream dreams. Where this is thwarted men become less than men. Part of their creaturehood has been taken away. The Christian should be the one who most clearly sees this in the modern scene where men are treated as less than men and the whole community and creation suffers.

"The creation is a symphony where we find a variety of creatures each singing the praises of the Maker in accordance with its unique character, different from creatures of another 'make.' The lion is to serve the Lord like a lion, the dandelion like a dandelion." (5) Men, alone in creation as the Image-bearer of God, can serve Him in their creativity. We are all capable of creative work, called not only to create after Him, but to encourage the gifts He has given others. As Christians we can even understand, appreciate and be enriched by the arts of those who are not Christian.

All Art can be Valuable

All artistic works are an expression of our common humanity, our creaturehood. They are a practical response to the way we are made and, like all God's gifts, are meant to be used to His glory. But it is a Fallen world and all man's faculties are corrupted by sin so it is part of sinful nature to seek to create things for our own glory or to an idol. Fallen men can corrupt the very gifts of God. This means, for the Christian, there is the danger that by condemning the way the gifts are used leads on to condemning the gift and ultimately the Giver. The gifts of God are good.

As Jesus taught, God is good to all men; He makes the sun to rise and shine on evil and the good and is kind to the ungrateful as well as the righteous. So the Creator God Who, moment by moment, upholds His creation and pre-serves it from the excesses of man's sin, also bestows gifts and abilities to men, believers and unbelievers, for the good of creation and the common good of humanity.

It is here we can see the value of the arts, even art created by those who confess themselves to be ungodly. God, in His 'common grace' has given gifts to the evil as well as the good. So although an artist may be in rebellion against God, a sinner who denies and defies God's Word and law, yet he is not an animal or devil – he remains a man, still stamped with the image of his creator. He still has his God-given humanity, moral and rational faculties and the ability to dream of things that never were and create things new and wonderful. So it should not be surprising that he can produce much that is true and beautiful.

In His grace, love and wisdom, God has endowed men and women with aesthetic appreciation, imagination, skill, craftsmanship and artistic ability so that, even in a sinful world, life may be illuminated by shafts of truth, splendour, hope and joy. Even ungodly art may be valid and important for a deeper and fuller understanding of personal and communal life.

Again, it was John Calvin who recognised this truth when he wrote: "Therefore in reading profane authors, the admirable light of truth displayed in them should remind us that the human mind, however much fallen and perverted from its original integrity, is still adorned and invested with admirable gifts from its Creator. If we reflect that the Spirit of God is the only fountain of truth, we will be careful, as we would avoid offering insults to Him, not to reject or condemn truth wherever it appears. In despising the gift we insult the giver." (6)

The truth of these words can be seen in our own century where men, profane and without knowledge of God's salvation, have revealed aspects of the truth of our age. Writers such as Kafka, Lawrence, Miller, Camus, Burroughs and Becket have shown in a brutal, yet often moving way, the agonies and predicament of modern man. Painters, sculptors and poets have all re-echoed the intense pain that has been disclosed in the theatre and serious cinema. They have shown the admirable light of truth in revealing aspects of life and society.

It is no task of the arts to deceive. As we have seen, this does not mean that art is a mere copying from nature or a realistic portrayal of what is perceived by the senses. Truth can be expressed through images, myths, and fictions. So the true portrait painter is not content to produce a passable likeness of the sitter; he is striving to portray the person behind the mask of the face, the true personality, the soul of the man. The true dramatist is not simply showing characters speaking and moving but tries, through words and actions, to reveal their deepest feelings and motivations as they face their problems and work out the conflicts. The poet, in creating images, emotions, rhythm and rhyme is digging beneath the surface to show the particular to be the universal, and the musician gathers sounds and harmony to explore new experiences. Art, as the highest form of craftsmanship, always transcends life, not to reduce it but make it more real by disclosing aspects unknown, ignored or forgotten. The arts are concerned with truth.

But how can a Christian know if a work of art is true? This is a real question in an age when, just as anything can be art, any position can be defended as true and truth. Indeed Picasso denied the very concept of truth. "What is truth? Truth cannot exist. If I look for truth in my canvas, I can do a hundred canvases with this truth. What, then, is the true one? And who is truth? The one who serves as my model or the one I paint? No, it's like everything else. Truth does not exist." (7)

In spite of such a statement, Picasso was one of the most prolific artists of all time; searching, experimenting, struggling, questioning, pursuing — what? If there is no truth then all thought, all questions, and even all art becomes a game without reason. There must be some criterion, some absolute, by which the value and truth of any statement can be judged, otherwise all intellectual inquiry and artistic revelations become mere matters of opinion.

The Christian knows that there is truth, a revealed truth against which all things can be measured. The truth of God's Word, written and incarnate. So the Christian is not compelled to use the same criteria as the humanist in his approach and judgement in considering the truth revealed in any work of art. The Christian does not measure all things according to reason, intuition, experience or chance — he can use these things but they are not the ultimate standard. God has revealed the truth concerning Himself, the world and humanity.

But the Christian, like all men, must first approach a work of art in an attitude of surrender, letting it speak and challenge. It is only after this attitude that a judgement can be made as to whether it is really worth such a surrender. Then, of course, the Christian can use the common tools of art criticism; being prepared to examine the form, style, technical excellence, intellectual and aesthetic content, intention and integrity, and the relationship between the style, form and meaning. But it is not enough to be critically aware that it is a well-written book, a dramatically-constructed play, an imaginative musical composition or a well-balanced, technically perfect picture. These are important, but for a Christian critique are not enough. There is a basic question which is often ignored in most art criticism today.

What is it saying? What is the basic statement, the root message being proclaimed by the artist? These are crucial questions in any Christian approach to the arts, for as we have seen, all works of art are a statement, a comment reflecting the artists world view and philosophy. So the question 'what is it saying?' is an important necessity for a Christian approach to any artistic production or artefact. It is in the answer to that question that the truth, or otherwise, may be found. The Christian, who knows the source of all truth, can accept works of art which disclose facets of the truth of life and reality. He can measure the proclamations of the arts against the revealed truth of God's creation, and the brute fact of sin. He can even rejoice in the possibility of redemption in Christ for a sin-cursed world. Above all, he can be truly thankful for the gifts of God to mankind in making creativity and the arts possible.

So the Christian does not have a narrow, bigoted view of the arts which can illumine and enrich his life. All things are his. Indeed he will recognise that, in the artistic and literary realms, it appears that the best gifts have been given to those who do not submit to Jesus Christ as Saviour and Lord. He appreciates, with Calvin, that "these radiations of Divine Light shone more brilliantly among unbelieving people than among God's saints". (8)

PART FOUR

THE CHRISTIAN USE
OF THE ARTS

10

THE ARTS AND THE CHURCH

There has always been a tension within the Church between the mystical 'other-worldly' view and an involvement in the affairs of men. From early in the Church's history there have been hermits and communities of monks who sought to escape from the snares and temptations of the world by withdrawing from all social contacts. These still exist in monasteries and among some pietistic, evangelical Christians who seek to live narrow, circumspect lives. Other Christians, down through the centuries, have seen their calling as being involved in politics, business, social action and in the arts. In the arts this tension has always existed and the attitude of the Church has fluctuated and often been vague and ambiguous.

In a famous and influential judgement, Pope Gregory the Great ruled at the end of the 6th century that: "The picture is to the illiterate what the written word is to the educate." (1) So the art of painting was accepted in the church as a means of telling the biblical story and revealing spiritual realities. Art was the picture book of the Bible.

Although the early Church Fathers condemned the theatre as the 'licentious representation of decadent paganism', theatres were such popular places of entertainment for the people that, even under Christian Emperors, it was found impossible to close them. But the immoral and brutal theatre of the Romans disappeared over the Dark Ages and it was from the Church a new form of drama came into being. Miracle or Mystery Plays developed from the liturgy used in services of worship. At Easter and Christmas the Gospels were read, often by two or more Priests, making it more realistic and dramatic. Additions were added to the text and versification crept in to intensify the story. Gradually cycles of these plays began to appear, dealing with all the great stories of the Old and New Testaments. If pictures were to teach the illiterate then drama was used to protray biblical history in an easily understood form.

As the medieval Church became more corrupt the arts became more secular. They had been the handmaid of the Church, though this was due to economic, cultural and social factors rather than to a theological principle. As the dominant authority, the Church controlled and influenced every aspect of the communal life in Western Europe. The Renaissance saw the arts becoming secular in subject matter and a revival of interest in the heroic period of classical Rome and Greece. Art, which once seemed tied to the apron strings of the Church, was increasingly seen as being able to stand alone.

The Reformation actually helped this separation between the Church and the arts and forged a new form of public worship which had little place for the arts of men.

Reformation View

It is generally taken as fact that the Reformation was hostile to all forms of arts and crafts; that it was a cold, austere, intellectual movement that sought to stamp out art and beauty and establish a grey conformity throughout Europe. Calvin particularly is seen as the bitter foe of art and aesthetic delight, showing not only a mere lack of interest in the arts but opposing them vigorously as the tools of the Devil. The truth is totally different.

John Calvin not only had a high regard for the arts in his thinking, but he encouraged his people to understand and appreciate the arts of men. They were, as a later Calvinist was to assert, 'one of the richest gifts of God to mankind'. (2) But the Church was not the sphere of the arts and the arts were not to be the handmaid of the Church.

So Calvin rejected the claim that images and representational art must be in the church as 'books for the unlearned'. This could only lead to idolatry and had no support from Scripture. The proper means of teaching and instruction was the preaching of the Word and the administration of the sacraments. The pagans had succumbed to the temptation of exaggerating the adornment of their temples but true godly beauty was not in decoration or images but in the spiritual life and unity of the believers. As the New Testament clearly teaches, true worship is coming to the Father in spirit and in truth.

Much of his criticism of the images in the Church were valid for his culture and age. Like Savonarola before him, Calvin condemned the artistic fashion of having saints painted in 'shameless luxury or obscenity' and complained that the inmates of brothels were 'more chastely and modestly dressed than images intended to represent virgins.' The fact that these were in Church buildings made them even more unacceptable. But he did not make a blanket condemnation of the plastic arts but wanted them to be used 'lawfully'. As he wrote:

"But, as sculpture and painting are gifts of God, what I insist on is, that both shall be used purely and lawfully, that gifts which the Lord has bestowed upon us, for His glory and our good, shall not be preposterously abused, nay, shall not be perverted to our destruction." (3) He wanted the arts to be used lawfully in their proper sphere. They are to be used for our 'instruction and admonition' not as vehicles of worship or preaching. The arts can enlarge our understanding of created reality, extend our experience and 'not least of all, bring delight to our hearts'.

Calvin had a strong regard for music, recognising it had Scriptural warranty in worship. Here again he knew the power of music which means it can not only uplift but debase. As in all his thinking it had to be God-centred. "The object of music is God and His creation. The glory of God and the elevation of man are its goal, and the inspired Psalms are its means. Since it is the goodness of God emanating through the universe that makes men sing, God ought to be the centre of man's thoughts and feelings when he sings. Seriousness, harmony and joy must characterise our songs to God." (4)

So music should bring glory to God and elevate our spirits and must be welcomed as 'one of the richest gifts'. It has an important place in the thinking of the Reformers – Luther at times wondering if his great love of music was not bordering on idolatry. There can be no doubt that music not only stirs the heart with originality and power but can lift the heart to God. It can bring tears to the eyes or create feelings of unutterable joy. It can stir emotions, create peace, love, tenderness and longing. Music can strengthen faith and lighten the dark night of the soul because by it, many, singing the praise of God have taken heart and renewed courage. The martyrs of the Church have died singing.

As in sculpture and painting, Calvin was deeply concerned that the art of music should be used purely and lawfully. Because of the 'secret and incredible power of music' there is the danger of being led astray. So Calvin warns: "music that degrades, that corrupts good manners, that flatters the flesh, must be rejected. For music has a secret and incredible power to move our hearts. When evil words are accompanied by music, they penetrate more deeply and the poison enters as wine through a funnel into a vat." (5)

So there was no romantic view that 'all music is sacred' or that the words do not matter. There is the recognition that we live in a Fallen world. Art, like all the gifts originally given for God's glory and the common good of mankind, can be used to glorify man and lead him to destruction. Calvin was aware that the human mind was a factory continually manufacturing idols and the peculiar power of the arts to influence and transform make them a dangerous force if used in the wrong way.

It is difficult, allowing Calvin to speak for himself, to see how he has earned the reputation of the arch-enemy of art, joy and beauty. In spite of his critics, Calvin did not have 'coldness stamped upon his brow' and in all his many writings shows no 'pathological hatred' of art or aesthetic delight. Even his actions deny the myth. On at least one occasion he supported the art-form most criticised by Christians – drama.

In 1546 a passion play was presented in Geneva with no objections from Calvin or his followers. The company presenting the play then asked permission to put on a miracle play which dramatised the Acts of the Apostles. The Genevan council asked Calvin for advice as to whether this play should be allowed and after reading the script and discussing it with other ministers he said it was 'sound and godly' and he would not oppose its production. When the play was first publically presented a fierce attack on it was made by Michal Cop and his opposition led to a riot which Calvin was called to quieten. Calvin calmed the people and players, but was angry with Cop, declaring that the 'poor man was in need of sounder sense and reason'. With Calvin's support, the play continued for another week.

So Calvin, as to a lesser extent Luther, sought to encourage the arts by defining their place and purpose. It was the misuse of the arts rather than art that was condemned. While removing the arts from the services of the Church they did not banish the arts as unworthy of Christian interest or involvement: But undoubtedly, Calvin severely limited the use of the arts in services of public worship, holding fast to the doctrine that the preaching of the Word and sacraments were to be paramount.

Reformed Worship

Compared to the rich liturgical drama of Roman Catholic and Orthodox services the Reformed tradition from Calvin has appeared austere and barren. Churches tend to be bare, there is a lack of colour and excitement, and public worship is more of an intellectual than emotional experience. The joy of the Lord is often overlooked in the searching for the 'deep things of God'.

The Westminster Confession of Faith states: "But the acceptable way of worshipping the true God is instituted by Himself, and so limited by His own revealed will, that He may not be worshipped according to the imaginations and devices of men, or the suggestions of Satan, under any visible representation, or in any other way not prescribed by the Holy Scripture." (6)

Scripture is the final authority in worship, as in all else, so only that which is in agreement with the Word of God should be allowed. It must be said that there is wisdom in this approach to public worship and it does seek to be true to the Word of God. The New Testament makes clear that the rich imagery and ritual of the Old Covenant passed away when Christ died, fulfilling the law and the prophets. The arts are not necessary for worship. God's people, those whom He has called, can worship Him in the fields, in caves, prisons or in their homes. They do not need highly-trained voices to sing His praises, poetically-shaped phrases to approach Him in prayer, or fine artistic gifts to offer to their God and King. All that is required is an approach in spirit and in truth.

There are dangers, in services of public worship, of introducing what the Westminster Confession calls 'the imaginations and devices of men'. The imaginative creations of art can become an end in themselves and be a barrier rather than an aid to worship. In a Church building it is possible to become so intoxicated with the glories of the artistic decoration, the colours and images of the murals, the lines of the sculpture, that the God who is to be worshipped is forgotten.

The same is true in the arts of music, poetry, drama and dance; the presentation can be so moving that it becomes something to admire in itself and for its own sake. So such services of worship can degenerate into a show where the congregation become spectators rather than participants in an act of worship. A choir, singing the Psalms to a glorious musical setting, or presenting a Bach Chorale, may indeed be worshipping by offering praise to God; or they may simply be singers enjoying the experience of creating music and harmony. Those who listen may, or may not, be caught up in a spirit of praise; they may simply be enjoying a musical performance. In all these things there must be the temptation to worship and respect the gifted artist and not the Giver of every good and perfect gift. The creature rather than the Creator is glorified.

So the reformed tradition in public worship has sought to discard all that would come between a man and his God. Worship and honour is due to God alone. But central to all this has been the sermon. Worship is not only being caught up in praise and adoration, offering our homage and reverence to God, but it is God speaking to us. God speaks to His people and the vehicle He has chosen is the 'foolishness of preaching.' The arts can have no place here as they are a creational gift and it is not their function to proclaim the Word of God in offering His grace and free offer of salvation in Christ. The proclamation of the Gospel is not the proper sphere of the arts within the creation.

Any critique of the Reformed tradition of worship must take account of three things which are important. These things show that it was not ignorance or bigotry that led to the removal of the use of the arts in worship. The Reformers were no more anti-art than they were anti-intellectual and the true tradition reflects this fact.

The first thing that must be said is that the Reformed tradition has sought to be faithful to the Word of God. They did claim a freedom, but it was a freedom with limitations. As there is no scriptural authority for images or pictures, drama or dance within the context of worship in the early Church, such things must be prohibited. And, as we have seen, there is wisdom as well as faithfulness in this approach; the arts can be a real danger to true worship.

Secondly, the reformed tradition of worship, by its very apparent austerity has a dignity and simplicity which has served many of the people of God well down the years. Indeed, one of the hallmarks of true art is an uncluttered simplicity, and the Reformed tradition has reflected this simplicity. It has led to a concentration on the essentials of worship rather than means. The centrality of the sermon has meant, not only an educated ministry but an educated laity; people were taught, not just to feel the truths of the Faith, but to understand them, to be able to 'give a reason for the hope that was in them'.

Thirdly, and this is often forgotten, the removal of the arts from public worship did not mean the discarding of the arts from all of life. As we have seen, Calvin is the most notable example here; he had a strong sense of the responsibility of the arts for the common good and it was this that governed his approach and appreciation. The arts of men may have no place in worship but they had a proper place in the world. The English Puritans had this attitude to the arts. Although, apart from the unaccompanied human voice, they forbade music in the Church, they encouraged music making in the home with the family gathered round the organ or enjoying violin or fiddle music. Such was their love of music that in the Commonwealth, under Cromwell, a Committee for the Advancement of Music was set up. And one of the greatest English Poets, Milton, was a Puritan. So the Puritans, in the Reformed tradition of refusing a place for the arts in worship, did not attack the place of arts in the world. It was the lewdness and decadence associated with the theatre that they objected to rather than the art of drama; similiarly they objected to dancing because of the lasciviousness associated with it.

So the Reformed tradition which has sought to be faithful to the Word of God, does have a meaningful dignified simplicity and has not always meant a discarding of the arts in all of life. But should the arts of men – themselves the gift of God – have no place in public worship? Can they not be an aid, though never a necessity, to worship?

The Arts in Worship

Of course there are arts used in the most non-liturgical service. Apart from the architecture of the building and the craftsmanship and colours of the furnishings, there is music, the poetry of the readings, the rhetoric of the prayers and sermon and some ritual performed. But, in spite of the dangers and temptations, is there not a need for a greater use of the arts? Properly used they can be an aid to worship and can create an atmosphere of reverence and praise. They can also bring a real challenge and demand a valid response.

The Bible does teach that, while our citizenship is in heaven, we are also creatures of earth. We are tied to the glory and burden of physical life. The things of earth have their own particular effect upon us — we are not purely spiritual beings whose sole function is to live on a spiritual plane. This is why the psalmist found comfort in lifting his eyes to the hills and why Jesus told his disciples to look at the lilies, sparrows, grass of the field — all part of the physical creation.

These things are not wrong. As Calvin himself asked: "Should the Lord have attracted our eyes to the beauty of the flowers, and our senses to pleasant odours, and should it then be a sin to drink them in? Has he not made even the colours so that one is more wonderful than the others? Has He not granted to gold and silver, to ivory and marble, a beauty which makes them more precious than other metals or stones? In a word, has He not made many things worthy of our attention that go far beyond our needs?" (7)

In spite of the sin that has corrupted all men the beauty of the earth can make hearts swell with thankfulness to the Creator. To those who are spiritually aware and awakened, beauty can bring them closer to God and create a sense of awe and worship. A sunset or sunrise; the moon reflecting on placid waters; a sparkling stream on a heather-clad hill or even the shining rain or flashes of lightning in a darkening sky can bring the awareness of another dimension transcending time and place. The arts can have the same effect. The echo of a few bars of music, some lines of poetry, the expression on a statue's face, a painting or a noble Cathedral can all touch the heart with wonder and awe.

So while recognising that the arts cannot be in themselves a diet of worship, or automatically lead to worship, there is the need to see afresh how they can be used to God's glory and the good of His people. They can make it easier for burdened and weary hearts to be lifted up and dimmed eyes to be opened to catch a glimpse of something of the glory and majesty of the God Who has made all things.

The image of the Christian Faith as seen by most people is expressed in the Church building. This tends to be grey, drab, old-fashioned and with little beauty. It seems to me that there is no good reason why our buildings and meeting places should be drab and colourless. After all, God is the God of beauty and glory; He is the Creator of the rainbow and the flowers, the multi-coloured sunset and the ever changing seas.

It must not be forgotten that the Church building is a perpetual witness to God in the world. "Architecture for churches is a matter of Gospel. A Church that is interested in proclaiming the Gospel must be interested in architecture, for year after year the architecture of the church proclaims a message that either augments the preached Word or conflicts with it . . . if the Gospel of Christ is worthy of accurate verbal proclamation week by week, it is also worthy of faithful architectural proclamation, where its message speaks year after year." (8)

Today men have forgotten the purpose of the Church spire and never look up; tied to the earth in a closed universe they never notice the spire pointing heavenwards. The Church building can be a perpetual witness that there is more to life than tower-blocks and industry, cars and motorways, concrete and asphalt. But Church buildings in decay, Churchyards over-grown with weeds, faded notices giving details of out-of-date events all carry their own message. They are a poor witness to the community of Christians who are called to bring the healing of the Gospel to all of creation.

Someone once cynically remarked that 'our Lord was first worshipped in a stable − in Scotland he still is'. But the bare churches of Scotland are not only an expression of poverty but culture − and simplicity has its own artistic appeal. There is no need for statues, murals, pictures and images − they can be a distraction. A single picture, a bare wooden cross, unobtrusive yet part of the worshipping environment, can serve as a focal point for the congregation and be an aid to worship. Too often, in reformed Churches, it is the organ pipes that dominate and a stranger might be forgiven for thinking that it is the organ that is the focal point of our public worship.

Music, of course, is widely used with its sister poetry. Many hymns, and certainly the Psalms, are poems set to music and this linking of words and music means that they become engraved in the mind and are easily recalled in memory. Most people can quote hymns learned in childhood easier than they can recall texts of the Bible. Words and music together make an excellent didactic tool.

Although a considerable number of 'Christian' musicals, hymns and choruses are being written today, many are poor poetry and equally poor theology. Doggeral mingled with a vague theology is not a suitable channel for praise to God or a help to the faithful. A good tune is never enough because the words, becoming engraved in the mind, become part of the theology and philosophy for Christian living. It is noticeable that the great hymnwriters − such as Watt, Wesley, Newton, Cowper, Bonar − wrote biblically based hymns which occasionally rose to the highest height of poetic expression. Many, if not most, of their hymns were little more than paraphrases of Scriptural passages and doctrines; not biblical phrases torn out of context, but poetically shaped commentaries.

Poetry is not confined to hymnwriting. It is a medium of the arts much used in the Bible and an excellent vehicle for communicating the truth. It seems to me that there is no good reason why it should not be used more widely in the life and worship of the Church.

A suitable poem could provide a call to worship or prayer, or even be used as a prayer in itself; many of the Psalms are poetic prayers. Poetry can give a dramatic opening to a sermon or climax the message with a challenge in a sharp concise way that demands a response. Poetry does have the power to cheer the downcast, comfort the bereaved and crystallise the hope that lies at the heart of the Christian Gospel. But it must be poetry that is worthy of the name of art.

Cheap, sentimental verses that are not true to life should have no place in the Church's worship or in the mature Christian's life. Victorian religious jingles and revival hymns may indeed create responses and arouse emotions, but it is at a superficial level; they do not speak to the heart with the intensity of true art. True art not only has the ability to create an immediate response but is capable of lodging in the heart and mind, revealing fresh insights as it germinates. A poem, which is the work of a true craftsman in words, is always fresh and relevant.

Drama was another medium used by the Prophets and, it seems to me, has something to add to services of worship. Biblical drama can be a help in understanding the historial reality of the Faith. The Christian Faith is historical, based on the God Who acted in history. So the dramatising of biblical incidents can serve by showing how these were experienced by real people in real situations. To be worthy they must be true to the source book of the Bible and not the fanciful interpretations dictated by the uncontrolled imagination of the dramatist.

Not only can biblical history be examined dramatically but contemporary problems could be fruitfully explored. Questions of individual and social morality, secularisation and the growing lawlessness of the age, indeed all of life, could be explored in drama. These would work out in practical concrete terms the problem and the relevance of the Christian approach, understanding and answer. But such drama, as in all Christian involvement in the arts, must be true to the art-form and to life as well as the Word of God. Romantic sweetness and glib answers must be avoided. The Greeks used the device of *deus ex machina* — the god who came down at the end of the play to resolve all problems. It is not a valid contribution to drama to substitute Christ for the *deus ex machina* and imply that all dilemmas and difficulties can be immediately solved by the acceptance of Christ and the Christian Faith. Such art is artificial. Life is not like that and the Bible does not give easy answers to all moral and intellectual problems in a world where all things are darkened by sin.

Drama, of course, can be more than verbal conflict; it can include mime and dance. Where these are sensitively used they can disclose fresh aspects of human experience and portray new ways of showing the goodness of God. Emotions are often too deep for words and the non-verbal arts of music and dance can express the inexpressible. Certainly they were widely used among the people of God in the recorded history of the Scriptures.

The arts can bring something of value to the services of public worship and can be exercised in obedience to the Word of God and be a genuine offering to Him. Public worship can use the fiction of drama, the created story, the poetic form, music and song to bring the people nearer to God and reveal facets of the truth He has given to men. Art can speak to the heart with power and conviction; it can fire the imagination and bring its own response which can be worked out in a life of service and praise. But it must be true art, the highest form of craftsmanship, finding its meaning in Christ and its service to God.

11

THE ARTS IN WITNESS

The arts are a witness, but not manipulation. They are propaganda, but not advertisements. An artist, whatever the medium he uses, is expressing his basic viewpoint, his philosophy, and by showing his work is seeking to convince others of the truth of his vision. He is making a statement and leaving it for others to consider and make their own response.

As all art reveals something of the faith of the artist, so Christian art will be rooted in the Christian Faith. This does not mean that such an art is limited to the Church or religious subjects and sacred themes. God is the God of all creation and the province and limits of the artist is that creation. He can be a servant of God as he writes, paints, shapes and composes according to the demands of his craft. There is Scriptural authority for asserting that even such mundane tasks as eating and drinking can be done to the glory of God.

So Christian art must not be a narrow branch of Christian apologetics defending the truths of the biblical revelation. "Art must never be used to show the validity of Christianity. Rather the validity of art should be shown through Christianity." (1) Christianity has a place for, and can justify, the arts in human life.

They are a gift of God and Christians have a duty and privilege to see that they are used aright. But the Church of the 20th century has inherited a Victorian religious romanticism which is a trivialisation of real art. It is a cosy little art style that makes no demands upon the intelligence and true sensitivity of those exposed to it. What is needed is a strong art which confronts the reality of life, affirming the Christian view of man's place and responsibility in the world. A comfortable art that does not disturb, challenge or deepen human life is a denial of the Faith that applies to every aspect of living. After all, the Bible – the Christian's textbook and guide – does not present an enchanting selection of refreshing stories or uplifting little homilies; it is concerned with the reality of life where men, in rebellion against God, destroy themselves, one another and the fair garden of creation. True art should do no less.

Perhaps a programme of education and re-learning is necessary before Christians can truly show the value of the arts in their witness and lifestyle.

Appreciating True Art

Men and women cannot live without art. Colours, decorations and ornamental artefacts are to be found in every home. Generally they are not works of real imagination and craftsmanship but a cheap pseudo-art; trivial sentimental products do have an appeal. But those immediately attractive pictures of children, sad wide-eyed little urchins looking with fear or curiousity at the world, are really stylised sentimental images of little value. They appeal to the emotions with an immediacy that deceives, creating sensations and arousing undefined nostalgic responses which offer nothing beyond their immediate appeal. To live with such pictures or objects is to find that rapidly they become commonplace and, after their immediate arousal of sympathy is forgotten, they have nothing to say. In a real work of mind and skill, which means true art, there is always something new, fresh and relevant. Pseudo art does not expand the vision, heighten percention, enhance reality, enrich human experience, nor is it a 'joy forever'.

But the very existence of these objects shows the need for art. People find it necessary to surround themselves with images and symbols to satisfy some deeper desire for beauty and meaning. So when they wish to express their deepest emotions, people naturally turn to some form of the arts. Dancing, music, hymns and songs are the most common expressions of joy. Then, as the 'Death and Memorial' columns of local newspapers show, poetry is used to demonstrate their grief and memories. More often than not it is a poetry that is scarcely removed from doggerel, but it demonstrates to reveal the feelings of their hearts, people instinctively turn to poetry — perhaps the language of the heart.

This natural desire for art, yet a lack of awareness or appreciation of the best, is also true within the Christian community. Here it is further complicated by the inheritance of the Victorian sentimentality that dominated 'Christian art' in the 19th century. This presented a false and glamorised reality that owed more to sentiment and romanticism than to truth. It was an art in which a 'sacred' fantasy ruled, not a biblical reality. Probably it is still true to say that for a great many Christians Holman Hunt remains the patron saint of 'Christian art.'

This art protrays a Jesus who was born in a clinically clean stable and was cradled in a freshly scrubbed manger. In Hunt's paintings fresh sweet-smelling straw covers the floor, hygienically pure-looking animals look on and in the background stand a Mary and Joseph, serene and saintly looking. The picture creates an atmosphere of pseudo-devotion that is far removed from real life. The glory and horror of the incarnation is lost in the cosy images of cheap sentimentality. This is carried over into the image of the man Jesus. Always he wears a spotlessly white robe never soiled by dust, his hair neatly groomed, and often surrounded by angelic looking children who are idealised into the Victorian concept of what children should be like.

But Christ, the Son of God, became a man and worked as a carpenter, he walked the dusty roads of Palestine and his friends were common people who did not have haloes round their heads or holiness stamped on their brow. He was not an effeminate character who lived in a warm haze of sentimentality, but a man, a real man living in a real world of real dirt and ugliness.

This presentation of cheap art affects more than the children of the Sunday School. Children grow up and art appreciation does not always mature. The truth of the matter is that most of us are haunted by the image of an idealised, sentimental Jesus who never had dirt on his hands or face or knew the sweat of labour on his brow. Such images are not only false to the historical record and truth of the incarnation but are a trivialisation of art by making it a vehicle for warm sentimental feelings that have nothing to do with reality.

It is not only the visual arts which are degraded in this way. Many mature, otherwise learned, members of the Church love with intense devotion the doggeral lines of gushing, warm-hearted sentimentality which are in many of the hymns of the last century. Many revere the cheap musical jingles and the 'Christian' fiction where the good is as 'good as can be' and the bad as 'bad as can be'.

While it is easy to condemn, the Christian must always be sensitive to the feelings of others and compassionate towards the weaker brother. Appreciation of the highest does not come automatically in life. It is only by being exposed to the best, by patient understanding and learning, that a true appreciation can begin to develop.

It is a fact that some of the greatest music ever written has been composed by devout Christians. The literature of the world has been enriched by Christian writers. Some hymns do achieve both poetic art and Christian confession. Painting, sculpture and architecture has flourished in Christian hands. Christians in the past have shown themselves to be artists no less fine than the most gifted of pagans.

Within the Christian community there should be an opportunity to learn of such things; to see something of the riches and treasures of the real art which is also part of our heritage. In almost every Church there are Youth Fellowships, Men's Clubs, Women's Guilds and other groups meeting for fellowship, teaching or simply recreation. Should there not be included in the syllabus items leading to a greater understanding of the gift of God in the arts? Teaching is needed here as in so many other areas of life. Allied to the teaching there could be an opportunity of experimenting and finding the limits and possibility of our common creativity.

Lord Reith wanted to run the B.B.C. on the principle that the 'people will respond to excellence'. Perhaps within Church organisations as people learn, discuss and experiment, an appreciation of the arts will be the response. But it is not enough to be aware of the rich Christian past in true art, or even to appreciate the best, there must also be encouragement for a Christian art in the modern world.

There is the need to encourage and support those with artistic gifts. The Christian community must seek to show to the world not only a good and strong art, but an honest one. This is the basic fault of Victorian sentimental art; it is dishonest. A dishonest art is a poor witness to a lost world.

T. S. Eliot faced this question. "Why, I would ask, is most religious verse so bad and why does so little religious verse reach the highest levels of poetry? Largely, I think, because of a pious insincerity. The capacity for writing poetry is rare; the capacity for religious emotion of the first intensity is rare, and it is to be expected the existence of both capacities in the same individual is rarer still. People who write devotional verse are usually writing as they *want* to feel, rather than as they do feel." (2)

This applies to all the arts. An art that is pretentious, self-conscious, artifically sentimental or cosily optimistic may be due to, as Eliot puts it, a 'pious insincerity'. Honesty is crucial in the arts and particularly in Christian poetry. The poetry of the Bible bears this out. The Psalmist expresses with complete frankness his sins, doubts, fears, hates and agonies as well as his trust, love and praise. Job freely gave vent to his despair and bewilderment and the Prophets often battered the very gates of heaven with their cries of distress and pain. They were totally honest in their art and the result is that their poetry is still relevant to our human experience.

An understanding and exposure to honest and true art will bring not only an enriched experience but restore the childlike sense of wonder that is so easily lost. Little children will pause and pick up strange, beautiful and even repulsive objects and examine them with fascination and wonder; they will examine with something approaching awe a petal, a leaf, a stone or even a spider and it will seem almost magical and miraculous. True art can have the same effect, making us rejoice with a deep sense of wonder at what we behold.

Encouraging True Art

In the modern materialistic world this sense of wonder is in short supply and imagination can become so fossilised that creativity is stunted. There can be no doubt that this is affecting our children. As toys become more realisitc there is less need for imagination. On television, programmes for pre-school children are less a stimulus to a child's imaginative and emotional development than sitting on mother's knee listening to a story. Children's programmes on the Media, even where they show educational and imaginative brilliance, can never replace the intense fun and excitement of a child playing with father where, through the magic of imagination, the carpet can become a jungle, a desert or a raging sea.

But it is not children alone who require to have their imaginations stimulated and their creative faculties developed. It is a need for all the family, and family life is impoverished where there is no room for dreams and all things are measured by economic necessity or material possessions.

As a contemporary economist has put it: "Precooked and packaged food-stuffs admittedly save the time of the busy housewife. But when a woman cooks for a man, or her family, is the activity only a chore? Or is there not also an instinctive satisfaction in feeding her man and her children – a symbolic giving of herself to them – an act of tenderness and affirmation? Children's television programmes can dispense with bedtime stories but does not the child who rests against his mother's breast and listens as the tale is gently unfolded, enjoy a richer experience? At the flick of a finger we can flood the living room with orchestral music that is perfectly executed, a delight to the ear – if we had not so much of it on easy terms that, unattentively, we hum snatches as we eat, talk, read or wash dishes. But before the turn of the century when the music a man could enjoy in his home might depend on his wife's skill at the piano or his daughter's singing, did not the performance also release some quiet springs of joy and sympathy between them?" (3)

So much of this is lacking in our hurried age and the mechanical reproduction of the arts are, at best, a poor substitute for being able to use and develop our own gifts. There is real joy to be found in the exercise of our own abilities and true delight in learning to appreciate the talents of others. Christians, knowing that all gifts come from God, have the special responsibility and privilege of seeing that gifts of heart and hand are creatively used and appreciated. Those with artistic talents should be prayerfully and practically supported particularly in an age of mass production and mass art.

In no age has life been easy for highly gifted craftsman, and the latter decades of the 20th century are no exception. In many ways, mechanisation and cost effectiveness increase the difficulties. As in all things, the personal touch is necessary for true human, and humane, living.

So while mass production and the artefacts of the mass society and mass art can have a place in the modern world, and can add something to life, they must not be allowed to dominate all facets of life. Christians, worshipping a God who created personality, and a unity with diversity and variety, must see through the brainwashing and manipulating techniques of the Admen, and the dangers in the pressures towards standardisation. They should recognise that they do not need to surround themselves with plastic gadgets and the cheap trinkets of machine-made pseudo art. Just as Christians are called to 'be not conformed to the standards of this world', so their homes should reflect a basic difference from those of the affluent, materialistic society of which they are part. They should prefer hand-made articles, items made with loving care by skilled hands that appreciate harmony and beauty.

There is a sense in which the home itself can become a work of art. Art, apart from the traditional meaning of craft, has many definitions and certainly it involves the bringing together of various elements; words, colours, forms, shapes, sounds, and other facets are merged together into a harmony where the whole becomes greater than the parts, and something new is created. Within this definition a home could become a work of art.

Furniture, furnishings, decorations, and all the necessities and bric-a-brac which make modern living comforting and pleasing, should blend together with an inner unity that expresses the taste and life-style of the family. There should be a totality of atmosphere and harmony, a creation of beauty where each member of the family can find his or her place as an individual, yet where the unity of the family is truly expressed. It should show something of the richness and beauty of a life lived before the face of the Lord. It would also show that the arts are for daily living and not the sole province of the intellectually snobbish.

Such a home would be a place where there was encouragement to read good literature, listen to good music, appreciate good art and where a healthy approach was made to the true value of the arts. It would be a place where there was room for the imagination and the things of the spirit. A place where, from the earliest days, children were taught to lift up their eyes and see beyond the mountains of possessions that are crushing the human spirit in the affluent western world of the 20th century.

Martin Luther, even with all the cares of the infant Reformed Church on his shoulders, still had time to exercise the imagination of his children. Away from home he wrote to his four-year-old son:

My Dearest Son,

I am glad to know that you learn well and pray hard. Keep on my lad, and when I come home I will bring you a whole fair.

I know a lovely garden where many children in golden frocks gather rosy apples under the trees, as well as pears, cherries and plums. They sing, skip and are gay. And they have fine ponies with golden bridles and silver saddles. I asked the gardener who were these children and he said, "They are the children who like to pray and learn and be good." And I said, "Good man, I too have a son, and his name is Hans Luther. Couldn't he come into the garden, too, and eat the rosy apples and pears and ride a fine pony and play with these children?" And the man said, "If he likes to pray and learn and be good, he too may come into the garden, and Lippus and Jost (*the sons of Melanchthon and Jonas*) as well; and when they all come together, they shall have golden whistles and drums and fine silver crossbows." But it was early, and the children had not yet had their breakfast, so I couldn't wait for the dance. I said to the man, "I will go at once and write all this to my dear son Hans that he may work hard, pray well, and be good, so that he too may come into the garden. But he has an Aunt Lena he'll have to bring too." "That will be all right," said he. "Go and write this to him."

So, my darling son, study and pray hard and tell Lippus and Jost to do this too, so that you may all come together in the garden. May the dear God take care of you. Give my best to Aunt Lena and give her a kiss from me.

Your Loving Father,
Martin Luther (4)

Children are naturally imaginative but although the practicalities of living soon crush the power of the imagination, no one ever really loses the ability to fantasise and daydream. All men and women are gifted with imagination. From this comes the spark that craftsmanship can turn into a work of art. As the dream becomes a reality, a work of art is born. Perhaps in the home, more than anywhere else on earth, can aesthetic sensitivity and artistic gifts be encouraged and allowed to develop.

But the Christian witness of the worth and validity of the arts should not be limited to appreciation and encouragement in the home and family lifestyle. There is, too, the community and the world.

Proclaiming True Art

Apart from enjoying and enriching their own lives by exposure to true art, Christians must show something of the value of the arts to the communities and soulless cities of our age. There is a desperate need to humanise our cities, and the arts have much to contribute.

Man, as an individual, was created to live in families and communities. He was made for a living environment, not for the machine city that depersonalises and separates him from creation and community. The fair garden of creation was not meant to be covered in concrete with asphalt for children to play on. Families were not created to be mere sociological units in an economic system but a living bond of people in relationship, not only to each other, but to the community and creation. The loneliness of the modern city, planned and shaped with shopping, industrial and dormitory areas, is a denial of community and spiritual health. The answer is not a Rousseau-like 'return to nature' or, as is happening, a flight from the inner cities of those who can contribute most. The answer is to humanise the cities, to make them for people.

Creativity can bring variety and excitement and the arts can bring something essentially human to the inhuman forces that are shaping our environment. What is needed is the opportunity for people to live to the full and to reach their potential.

In seeking to break away from the destructive mould of mass conformity, many are engaged in a search without a goal — looking for they know not what. There is the fanaticism of football supporters and the false hopes raised by the betting shop. Pubs and clubs are crowded with those seeking identity and community; bingo halls offer cheap fellowship and endlessly, there is the flickering television screen offering the illusion of mindless escape. Another way must be found.

A problem remains, as William Morris recognised over a century ago: ". . . civilisation has reduced the workman to such a skinny and pitiful existence, that he scarcely knows how to frame a desire for any life much better than that he now endures perforce. It is the province of art to set the true ideal of a full and reasonable life before him, a life to which the perception and creation of beauty, the enjoyment of real pleasure that is, shall be felt to be as necessary to man as his daily bread, and that no man, and no set of men, can be deprived of this except by mere opposition which should be resisted to the utmost." (5)

Christians, awakened to the rich gift of the arts, should be in the vangaurd of a movement to bring the 'perception and creation of beauty, the enjoyment of real pleasure' to all. So there would be great value in Christians being involved and encouraging the arts and cultural activities of the community. It would be a worthy witness and an opportunity to exercise their calling to be salt and light in an area of communal life where these necessities have been lacking.

So youth theatres and community drama could be supported; local artists could be encouraged to put on local exhibitions, and poets and writers helped to have their work read and published. Many towns and areas are establishing, or resurrecting, 'Gala days' and local Festivals of the Arts are becoming annual events. Rather than importing professional companies, they might well arouse greater local interest if they were purely community festivals. Something of the common work could be shown; paintings, sketches, photographs, floral arrangements and all the arts and crafts. Groups could come together to present music, song, poetry and drama.

Christians involved in this, or specific Christian groups, could bear excellent witness as the community is brought together to celebrate its common humanity. Local congregations could have something to contribute to such festivals and there could be a judicious use of Church buildings to encourage the realisation of the creative riches that are in any community. Perhaps even local congregations could take the lead in these areas; a Festival of Christian art.

But such activities call for more than dedication; they require some real and hard work. Perhaps for too long Christians have been content to be poor copies of non-Christian artists, and with sympathetic and non-critical audiences, have presented second and third rate productions. 'It is for the Lord, He will bless it' is a poor prayer when anything shoddy or trivial is created and presented. Art is craftsmanship and that entails hard work and real effort. Nothing worthwhile was ever made without effort.

The arts are a witness and a proclamation, part of our humanity and creaturehood. They can disclose the truth and bring joy to the heart. Because they have been given by God Christians have the responsibility of seeking to encourage their use by being involved and appreciative. But, of course, Christians cannot blindly support all that claims to be art just as they cannot believe all that claims to be truth.

The Christian community cannot encourage or support the celebration of evil or sexual titillation; it cannot praise an art that proclaims that chaos, chance or meaninglessness is king. It is no calling of the Christian to encourage the arts if they are seeking to build a better, more artistically designed Tower of Babel. But, as we have seen, the Christian is free to learn from all – because all gifts come from God, even when they are misused and perverted. Even in unchristian and anti-Christian art there is the possibility of dialogue and constructive criticism.

What is needed is not just condemnation or censorship but a better way. The challenge is:

"That men of darkened understanding can make merry under God's nose and curse Him with desperately, damnably forceful art should hurt you.

God is not dead: Christ lives! Man is not absurd: he glories in the image of God! The world is not a curse: it is a good creation, struggling under sin towards final deliverance! And only different art, not censorship, will take this antithesis earnestly and meet it." (6)

12

THE CHALLENGE OF THE ARTS

The arts are in a state of crisis. "Like science, art has become remote from living: it is not, as . . . in primitive societies, an integral part of our culture, existing in all aspects of life, in everyday matters, in religion. Art has become separate and specialised, understood only by a minority, segregated in galleries, museums and concert halls, and, like science, exploited for political and commercial ends." (1)

The Fine arts have become remote, divorced from the communal life of the community and often beyond any rational understanding or aesthetic appreciation. There is much in the art galleries, theatres, concert halls and libraries that cannot be art in the true meaning of the word. Only total irrationality could accept the word 'sculpture' to apply equally to a collection of firebricks and Michelangelo's 'Pieta'. It seems completely unreasonable to consider the works of Shakespeare and Milton as being on the same level as something like 'concrete' poetry where the shape of the words on the paper is more important than the content. Then 'minimal art', where the canvas − often blank − is the art object, cannot really be compared to the works of Rembrandt, Constable, or even Van Gogh. Art without craft can become meaningless.

It is a world where "our culture is breaking down. If any confirmation is needed go to the films, read the books of today, walk round a modern art gallery, listen to the music of our time − hear, see, open your eyes and ears to the cries of despair, the cursings, the collapse of this world." (2) That is the verdict of a Christian art historian, but the same opinion is being echoed by many humanist artists of our age. As a major European dramatist has put it: "Our so called culture seems nothing but a house of cards. There is a question mark over everything." (3)

How, then, can Christians respond to the challenge of the arts in our age? Perhaps the starting point should be tears. Weep for a glorious gift that is being degraded and corrupted into a worthless thing; for art that shows no craftsmanship and communicates no vision. Weep for our theatres where blasphemy and sexual license are mistaken for liberty; for our often violent and pornographic cinema; for cheap sensational literature; for poetry that has nothing to say; paintings revealing no created reality, and music that only disturbs and can never delight. We must weep for our lost culture, for the makers of that culture and the casualties that are all around us. We must mourn for the death, and apparent death, of real art that, made with skill and imagination, can reveal a transcendant reality adding fresh dimensions to human life.

The tears should lead to prayer. Prayer for those highly gifted that they will use their talents to enrich human life, bring truth and joy by opening our eyes and understanding. We should pray for those whom God has called to serve Him in the arts that they might learn to use then aright in their lonely, difficult and yet glorious calling. Above all, we should pray that God, the giver of every good and perfect gift, will raise up Christian artists for our age; men like Bezalel and Oholiab who, called to work on the building of the Tabernacle, were 'filled with the Spirit of God, with ability and intelligence, with knowledge and all craftsmanship'.

But Christian response to the contemporary challenge of the arts should not end with tears and prayer. There must be involvement by offering a real alternative; Christians must accept the challenge by being contemporary, relevant and yet remain faithful to their Lord.

The Challenge to be Contemporary

Christians, in their understanding and contribution to the arts, must be contemporary. In this they face real problems. In almost all the arts there has been no continuing Christian tradition on which to draw; by largely withdrawing from the culture, Christians of a previous generation have ensured that growth and development in the arts have been left in the hands of those who owned no allegiance to Christ. There can be no going back to an 'age of faith' or a use of the same techniques and forms. Art, to communicate today, must be in the visual and verbal language of the 20th century.

So the Christian artist cannot, and should not, go back to the time when it was acceptable to present morality plays, paint romatically glossy biblical pictures, or compose 'religious' oratorios. Milton's literary style is not the only possible way for a Christian to write poetry and a Christian novelist should not blindly follow the pattern set by John Bunyan. Painters do not need to accept the style of Rembrandt or Hunt as the only acceptable way for a Christian artist, and musicians, anxious to serve their Lord with their music, are not bound to the style of Bach, Handel or Haydn. Morality, Miracle or Mystery plays are not the Christian necessity for the contemporary stage.

The Christian – like all men – can learn from the past but he should not be a prisoner of it. It is a fact that, "we must know what is going on, and understand our environment if we want to achieve anything of relevance to our times. We must know the spirit of our times in order to know where it is wrong and should be challenged and fought." (4)

To know the 'spirit of the age' is to recognise that all contemporary art is not an intellectual practical joke or a deliberate deception. The arts of our age are not all trivial products designed merely to deceive, shock or titillate. The modern dramatist is not necessarily playing idly on the unconscious fears of humanity when he writes plays for the Theatre of the Absurd; he may sincerely believe that life is indeed absurd and should be exposed. The Abstract artist who deliberately destroys form and shape may genuinely feel that these things have departed from the world and it is an act of illusionary nonsense to try and retain them. Anti-melodic music, poetry which is sound without sense – confusion without conviction – sculpture that is shape without form, and novels without beginning, middle or end, may all be the sincere expressions of genuine artists striving to reveal the real world of the 20th century. Often they are presenting painful images and myths which express powerfully the reality of life in a world where meaning and hope appear to have departed. They are a mirror to the 'spirit of the age.'

In previous ages the Christian Faith dominated Western civilisation giving the base for a Christian culture. Not that all artists, or intellectual leaders, were Christians, but they did work within a Christian consensus and world-view. With the decline of the influence of the Christian faith has come confusion, complexity and fragmentation because there is nothing to hold all things together. George Orwell, who was not a Christian, asserted in 1944, 'One cannot have any worthwhile picture of the future unless one realises how much we have lost by the decay of Christianity'. (5) The picture is clearer now than when he first wrote those words and the arts reflect the difference in their retreat from rationality and meaning.

The Christian – who is called to move with God and not necessarily with the times – can still be contemporary in his art. He can learn from the past and the present expressions of the arts and speak to modern man in a language he can understand. While he is not called to preach the Gospel in his art, the Christian artist can be contemporary if he asserts two things that are true to his Faith and the need of man – the value of art and the value of man.

The arts are more than butter on the dry bread of life; they are not a mere entertainment, an escape from harsh reality. They can entertain and delight, they can add excitement to the drudgery of living, but they are a necessity and a blessing. They are a gift of God and should be enjoyed to the full. In an age of spiritual deprivation, the crushing of the human spirit by crass materialism, the arts will speak to the deepest longings of modern man when they are shown to be of worth for true life and living.

So paintings should be more than pigment sprayed on to canvas; they should disclose aspects of the truth that can be seen in landscape, still life, portrait or imaginative creations. Drama should be more than a vehicle for socialist or humanist propaganda, or to display existential despair or romantic hope; it should be a revelation as to how human beings can cope with perplexities and problems while holding on to their dignity and humanity. Music, recognised perhaps by all as the greatest gift, should not be a means of reducing man to a mere emotion, making him into a frenzy of response to beat and rhythm; it should, in Calvin's words be recognised that 'among the other things which are suitable as a means of recreation, and of giving pleasure, music has a primary place'. (6) Creative literature should be more than an escape from life but a unique means of enlarging experience by revealing the depth of human emotion and sensitivity. The arts are not given to titillate sensual appetites and degrade human instincts.

So the Christian can be contemporary by asserting the proper place and importance of the arts for all. They were not given by God for the benefit of the select few, for an aesthetic élite, but for the edification and joy of all mankind.

The Christian, alone in all modern philosophies, can show the worth and importance of the individual. Man as the image-bearer of God; made a 'little lower than the angels' – Pascal's 'ruined archangel.' The Romantics wanted man as a god. Probably their greatest hero is the image, created by Byron, of Count Manfred standing in the splendid solitude of the Alps, shaking his fist at God. But the Romantics failed in their view of man. In Goethe's *Faust* the hero sells his soul to Mephistopheles that he might gain all experience and power – then uses it to seduce a simple village maid – Gretchen. Man could not be a god.

But equally man is not the nothing portrayed in much contemporary art; he is not the faceless nonentity of contemporary painting or the soulless character of much modern literature. He is not an unprogrammed computer in the technological world or the helpless being trapped in the existentialists' concept of time.

The Christian can be truly modern when he shows contemporary man his true self in a mass world. A creature, made in the image of God, great and yet flawed with sin. A being, rational and moral, important in the eyes of

God, and of eternal worth. The arts, in portraying that, will be truly speaking to contemporary man at the depth of his need. The Christian artist does not need to be old-fashioned in showing that there is an alternative to the drugged despair that lies at the heart of so much modern art.

The need to be contemporary implies that there must be experimentation. Just as great art always comes from much art — Shakespeare was not the only dramatist in Elizabethan England and Michelangelo was not the only artist in Florence — so Christian art to be contemporary must come from many attempts and even failures. There is no sin in trying and failing. So the challenge to be contemporary must mean the welcoming of possibilities, trying, striving, experimenting and working without fear of failure. In learning from the past and the best of the present the Christian can seek to speak to modern man in a language he can understand.

The Challenge to be Relevant

A great amount of what passes for modern 'art' today seems totally irrelevant to the real business of living for the vast majority of people. But the arts, if they have anything to contribute to human life, must be relevant. So Christians, if they are to be involved in the arts, must seek to be relevant, not only to the age but to the human condition and understanding.

The 20th century has seen a flight from rationality. The Fine Arts, once known as the 'beautiful arts' have largely degenerated into meaningless pictures and sounds, producing confused images and esoteric symbols. It is not surprising that the arts have become a minority interest and their insights and delights are only available for the few. The mass man is given the forgetfulness of pleasure for his spiritual poverty and human deprivation. The arts appear to have become irrelevant.

The majority of people do not crowd into the theatres, visit modern art galleries, queue for the concert halls, memorise contemporary poetry or study the works of the serious and thoughtful writers of the age. Pleasure-seeking has become the governing ethos of Western man — a search for a pleasure that brings no disturbance; a binge without a hangover, a drug trip without coming back to reality or the ultimate orgasm giving eternal ecstasy. In this situation the arts, to appear relevant, must first of all — and perhaps also finally — be entertaining. This is a path which many gifted people have taken, gladly selling their talents for the flickering fortune of the mass media or in humble obedience to the dictatorship of the pop charts.

So it is a world where pop music drives out the pain of thought for the young; the trivia of television hypnotises the old, and a man's life is seen as consisting in the abundance of his possessions. The old Neroian principle of 'bread and circuses' is re-enacted. The technically-organised welfare state provides the bread and the mass media supply the circus – everyone should be happy and content.

In an age of frantic and frenzied enthusiasm for pleasure and escape, amid the noise and the nonsense, the emptiness and futility, how can a Christian art be relevant? The answer lies in accepting the challenge that "unbelievers revel in music and drama, painting, poetry and dance, with a riot of colour, a deafening sound raised in praise to themselves and their false gods. How can you live here openly and silently? Are you satisfied with bedlam for God? Where is our concert of freshly composed, holy stringed music? Our jubilant dance of praise to the Lord? What penetrating drama have our hands made? Why do we not break into a new song, not one from our slender archives? This is needed to show our God that we love Him here too, passionately." (7)

If the Devil has the best tunes the answer is not to steal his but to write better ones. Only the Christian can know the true triumph song of life and death. All things are his and he has no need to be a religious bigot imprisoned within a narrow theological cell. He can be relevant by showing true joy, true life and true hope. Alone of all men he should know praise and thanksgiving and rejoice in all the rich gifts which the Heavenly Father has freely given to His children.

The Evangelical Awakening under Whitefield and Wesley in the 18th century unleashed a wild wave of religious hysteria and uncontrolled enthusiasm throughout the country. It was irrational and disturbed the leaders. But Charles Wesley, with the arts of poetry and music, channelled that enthusiasm into a passion for hymn-singing so that a new form of religious art captured the hearts of the people and eventually changed the pattern of public worship throughout the churches. His work was relevant and lasting.

But a true Christian involvement in the arts must not seek simply to baptise current trends into the faith but confront the world with visions of reality. Escape from problems does not lead to solutions. As the serious secular artists of our age are finding, it is difficult to speak when no one wants to listen, and hard to try and reveal visions to those who do not want to see. It is a challenge to be relevant and truthful and Christians, least of all, cannot refuse that challenge.

One of the functions of a Prophet was to tell the world about itself; to show things as they really are. Artists are not prophets in the biblical sense of the word, but they do have, with their sensitivity and insight, the ability to see things truly. They can often reveal the secrets of their own heart and it becomes a mirror held up to reflect the reality of their own age.

This is why T. S. Elliot's poem, *The Waste Land*, published first in 1922 created a great deal of interest then and, having been rediscovered by contemporary students, is still the fascinating subject of debate and discussion. Certainly it is significant in that it broke away from the conventional use of poetic language by using foreign phrases, incongruous imagery, historical references and an almost complete lack of narrative sequence. Yet in spite of the obvious difficulties, the poem speaks to modern man because it expresses the heart of contemporary man.

The Waste Land portrays a world where passion, lust, sympathy and feeling are all gone; April may breed lilacs out of a dead land but nothing grows from the dead heart of men. There is only dry rock and no water — nothing to fertilise or refresh the barren world. Certainly the rich still have their luxury but within their heart is only the cancer of boredom. The poor are equally empty, longing for a good time while the idle chatter is punctuated by an insistent voice declaring, 'Hurry up please, it's time'. Time for all things to end but the end can bring no relief, no redemption; only a decaying, twilight world where even the echoes of hope are lost. Throughout the poem distinct echoes of pagan and Christian religious thoughts are expressed, but they are not developed, they are but the memories of a past that is as dead as the painful present.

The poem was more than the cry of Eliot, an individual poet; it was a sob of the human heart, conscious of spiritual starvation, crying in the 'waste land' of the 20th century. It was the voice of modern man finding himself in a world where all the old foundations had gone and nothing remained but ghostly echoes to haunt and torment. Eliot showed the world of the 20th century by revealing his own agony; he showed the world itself. It was painfully relevant.

Christians have the continuing challenge to be relevant in the age in which they are called to serve. By the imaginative use of the arts they can disclose the truth in fresh, exciting and challenging ways. The truth is that there is joy, celebration and ecstasy in life, but there is also sin, guilt and judgement; that life does not have neat beginnings, patterns and ends, but that behind and above all things there is a God who made the world, loves the world, and sent His only begotten Son into the world . . ..

But Christian arts will only be relevant when they can confront the world, not as a tool of emotive evangelism, a branch of apologetics, or a special form of preaching, but as real art. Art which is concerned to be true craftsmanship, ever seeking to extend the possibilities of the gift that has been given. The arts, made in obedience to God and in intent and content, are meant for His glory will always be relevant.

The Challenge to be Faithful

Christians are called to be faithful in all things; artists are no exception. This means that the arts must be an expression of his Christian faith and created in obedience to the Lordship of Christ. As Paul wrote "Whether therefore ye eat or drink, or whatsoever ye do, do all to the glory of God." (1 Cor. 10.31.) The Christian is a man under authority, commanded to work 'in all things' to the glory of God. In fact he has a patron.

The humanist artists rejoiced at the ending of the old system of patronage where they had to produce works of art according to strict specifications laid down by the patron. It seemed that the ending of patronage would herald a new freedom to experiment and expand the language and use of the arts in society. This freedom proved illusionary. Artists have had to adapt to what is merely fashionable and allow public taste to dictate what should be produced; or they have succumbed to the patronage of the ad-men, using the gifts of creativity and craftsmanship to sell soap powders or plastic baubles. Those who have tried to remain true to their own artistic vision have often ended up merely as members of artistic cults, creating art for one another and removing art from the everyday life of the community. Instead of being the voice of society they no longer communicate to the world of ordinary men and women.

The contemporary artist, in seeking total freedom in the name of his art, has found that this can lead to a new bondage. Unrestrained art can degenerate into anti-art and end as anti-human. If the mass man of the technological society has become so dehumanised, and desensitised, that ordinary scenes of pain and distress do not shock him, then the temptation is to become more horrific to get a response. This is the slippery slope many artists find themselves on.

As a spectacle, a circus is improved with wild lions – would it not be more dramatic if real Christians were thrown to those lions? Indeed for the first time since the fall of the Roman Empire the sex act is now performed, or simulated, on the public stage, and this has been greeted as an artistic breakthrough. Films which depict in graphic detail, often in multicolour and slow motion, scenes of rape, brutality and murder are now commonplace and the devaluing of language with crude swearing and casual blasphemy are familiar to readers of modern fiction or to contemporary viewers of television. Increasingly, in the name of a mythical freedom, artists are being compelled to cater to the lowest common denominator. Freedom has become license and liberty reduced into anarchy.

The arts, in their search for freedom in the contemporary scene, have probably produced more problems than masterpieces. Freedom, without restraint or restriction, is an illusion; life itself, with the limitations of the creational structures, sets boundaries that no man can break. There is the well-known story about Thomas Carlyle who heard of a woman who claimed that her basic philosophy was that she 'accepted the universe'. Carlyle commented, "Gad, sir, she'd better!"

It is supremely the Christian who should know that freedom is only possible under law. *Lex rex* – 'law is king'. There is liberty, but there are also limitations; there is freedom, but there is also responsibility. The Christian faith is concerned with individuals and society, with community and the cosmos. There is a place for the arts within, art that is undertaken in faith and is an expression of that faith. It can be part of the 'all things' that have to be done 'to the glory of God'. As Calvin has reminded us, "All craftsmen, of whatever kind, who serve the needs of men, are ministers of God." (8)

The arts do serve the needs of men. And Christian art, even in an age of faithlessness, can be an affirmation of faith. It could restore faith in the arts themselves as a valid medium with a valuable role to play in the community of men; stimulating awareness, encouraging sensitivity and, not least of all, giving a pure pleasure and great delight. It could help to re-establish the world-view that, behind the riches and diversity of life, there is a unity that holds all things together; a transcendent reality that is not dependent upon irrationality or an illogical mysticism. Above all, Christian art, could show that there is not only meaning, harmony and purpose in the universe, but that there is the possibility of redemption; while it would reveal the creation groaning in travail it would speak of the healing possible now and the coming restoration.

But Christian art, as works of craftsmanship and faith, should have a glorious ambition. "There must be a science which will not rest until it has thought out the entire cosmos; a religion which cannot sit still until she has permeated every sphere of human life; and so also there must be an art which, despising no single department of life adopts, into her splendid world, the whole of human life, religion included." (9)

So Christian involvement in the arts should not be the cosy activity of a comforting few for the Christian ghetto. Neither must it see itself as one branch of art among the many schools and systems. Rather it must strive to permeate the whole culture, contributing to every facet of human life and society. It must be a salt to preserve that which is good and wholesome; a true light to illuminate and illustrate that which is in the dark.

The biblical promise is that the King will return and establish His Kingdom. Then all things will be restored and will find their true fulfilment in service and praise. Meanwhile, as citizens of that Kingdom, Christians are called to exercise their gifts knowing that nothing worthy will be lost for, in that day in the New Jerusalem, "they shall bring into it the glory and the honour of the nations." (Rev.21:26. RSV)

Until that day of restoration:

Let us sing of the mercies of our God
And make His Name known in all our ways.

He has created all things for His glory
And given the world as a place for our delight.
There is the strong quietness of the hills
And the music of sea and air;
The comforting warmth of the sunshine
With the shining rain for refreshment;
Even the dark blackness of night
Is studded with stars.

As creatures of creativity
We can dream dreams
And with heart and hand, shape those dreams
To celebrate the joys of creation.
With imagination and intuition
We can imitate and create,
Making fictions and fantasies
To bring forth something of the truth,
And the wonder of created things.

Beauty and splendour
Are gifts from His Hands,
Comfort and curiosity
Are among the blessings He has bestowed.
The very desire for form and meaning,
The craving for the sublime,
These have been placed in our hearts
By the God Who made all things possible.

Let us remember the grace of our God
Who is the giver of every good gift;
Who, even in a sinful world
Still gives music, poetry, drama,
And all the arts and crafts of men

To illumine and instruct the humble heart,
And bring delight to the souls of men
By giving shape to their praise.

Let us sing of the mercies of our God
And the gifts He has given to the children of men.

THE END

APPENDIX

Scotland, Calvin and the Arts

Some Preliminary Observations

There is a need for research and historical study into the complex subject of the influence of Calvin on the arts in Scotland. In spite of the exaggerated claims of some critics, Scotland has a rich cultural history and has produced much of value in music, poetry, literature and the other arts. It is not enough to accept uncritically the common mythology that all that is evil in the Scottish culture, and all that is bad in the Scottish character, is due solely to John Calvin and his puppet, John Knox. Only a naive view would see Scottish history as a saga of Calvinist theology; political, economic and social forces have also been involved in shaping the nation's culture and character.

Historically there have been at least two Scotlands—Highlands and Lowlands; each with its own language, traditions and cultures. Certainly, as the history of the land developed, the Lowlands became dominant in creating the Scottish character, but the old Celtic and Highland strain cannot be ignored. Then, while Calvinism strongly influenced the Scottish culture, there was also a corrupt form of Calvinism. There has been the perversion of Calvinism as illustrated by Burns' 'Holy Willie' and James Hogg's *The Confessions of a Justified Sinner*, and a negative Puritanism which denied the value of earthly pleasures and owed more to the worst forms of pietism than to Calvinism.

While acknowledging these factors it remains true that Calvinism, as a theology and philosophy – and it is both – has been the dominating force in making Scotland. But, particularly in the arts, has it been totally detrimental to our cultural history? Has Calvin indeed been responsible for the dearth of artistic talent? Or – a sometimes forgotten question – has the dearth been as bad as it is sometimes made out? Being neither a historian or theologian I can only offer some preliminary observations and raise some general, but pertinent and relevant questions.

Scotland and Calvin

Scotland is a land of legends, so that sometimes it is difficult to know where the truth ends and the myth begins. Often our history seems only a nostalgia for a misty past that never existed; a past that can be conjured up by a word or phrase. Emotions surge in the Scottish breast at the mention of Wallace, Bruce, Bannockburn, the Declaration of Arbroath, Flodden, Covenanters, Bonnie Prince Charlie, Glencoe, Rabbie Burns – they all have the force of a myth that transcends factual history. But perhaps the strongest emotions are aroused by the name of John Calvin. It has become more than a name; it has become a race memory, a myth and a legend to haunt and torture.

Scotland, as Sydney Smith once remarked, is a 'land of Calvin, oatcakes and sulphur'. Always it is Calvin who comes first. The name evokes the picture of a cold, cruel hand hanging over the fair land of Scotland, descending to crush out all joy and pleasure in living and denying the pursuit of art and beauty. Scotland is seen as a prison, with Calvin the jailor.

Against this myth must be set the fact, often forgotten, that Calvinism was not imposed upon the Scottish people. In Scotland, more than in any other country in Europe, the Reformation was a popular movement. It was not imposed by Court, by nobles, by the bourgeoisie or by invaders; indeed the people had to rebel against Court and civil authorities to establish the kirk. Calvinism rather than Lutherism captured the souls, heart and mind of the Scots, and the Reformation was probably more far reaching in depth and range in Scotland than in any other country. Apart from the work of God in calling a people back to a biblical Gospel, could it not be argued that there was something in the strict logic, mental and moral discipline of Calvinism which eminently suited the Scottish character? It did come through assent.

Did this then mean the death of artistic culture and aesthetic pursuits? Again it is difficult to separate fact from myth. There is a certain dramatic attraction in the myth of a pleasure-loving, artistically gifted people being choked to death by the grey mist of Calvinism. But the implication of such a myth is that historically, Scotland was always a land infinitely rich in potential but frustrated artists. That, without Calvinism, Scotland would have given the world, for generation after generation, artists, musicians, dramatists, poets, writers and an endless variety of artistic genius of every description. It implies that our nation was forever full of 'mute, inglorious Miltons' who could not sing because of the prohibitions of Calvinism.

If such a thesis is true then it is in plain contradiction to the fact that no nation, irrespective of its theological of philosophical foundation, has produced great art for generation after generation and century after century. Even if it were true, is John Calvin to blame? As I hope this book has showed, by allowing Calvin to speak for himself we find he had a healthy respect for the arts, seeing them as a gift of God which must not be despised. If Scotland was anti-art then I would suggest that the blame cannot be laid at the teachings of John Calvin.

One argument in favour of the negative view of the arts in Calvinist Scotland is the fact that we did not produce a theatre. Ramsay's attempt to found a theatre in 18th-century Scotland failed mainly through the opposition of the Church, and John Home, who wrote a greatly acclaimed but now forgotten play, was forced to resign from the ministry. It must be admitted that many Calvinists, like the Puritans, were suspicious of the theatre on moral grounds, but Calvin, as we have seen, did not condemn drama totally.

Another question arises. Considering the history of Scotland, it is surprising that she did not produce a theatre? It was a small nation with a limited population and the greatest events in life and death were enacted not on stage, but in the open. Great disputes and conflicts did indeed take place, battles were fought from pulpit and General Assembly, books and pamphlets flooded the land and at times it seemed that everyone was involved. Often these debates and disputes ended in secessions, separations and even violence. Often the future of Church and nation was decided in public. What dramatist could hope to rival the dramatic events and intense emotions of the Covenanters and the 'killing times'? What writer could imaginatively conceive the brave curtain-speeches of the condemned? Considering our history, is it too fanciful to suggest that Scotland produced no theatre because the whole land was a stage and the Scots were not docile spectators but participants?

The myth of Calvinism being the death of the arts leaves one question which I have never seen discussed. In the Europe of the 16th and 17th century, the two most Calvinist countries were Holland and Scotland. It is obvious that the arts, and in particular the visual arts, flourished in Holland under a Calvinist culture. So can Calvinism be responsible for an artistic renaissance in the Netherlands and an artistic dearth in Scotland?

Education and Calvinism

Apart from the primitive arts, usually associated with 'magical religions', it requires a measure of education to appreciate truly the arts. It seems to me that there can be no denying that Calvin did give Scotland her high regard for learning which must lead to an understanding and appreciation of the arts. Certainly Calvin recognised, and his followers in Scotland accepted, that it was essential that people should be educated or they would not be able to sustain an enlightened Christian faith.

So at the Reformation in Scotland the Book of Discipline gave an imaginative scheme for universal education at every level. Within the context of the 16th century it was a glorious vision completely unknown in any other nation. It proposed a national, compulsory system of schooling with a school in every parish, a college or secondary school in every major town, and the Universitites in the principal cities. Education was to be freely available for all who could take advantage of it.

Although the schools, colleges and Universities were to be under control of the Church it was not proposed that only a narrow theological education should be given. Indeed it eventually led to the Scots 'lad o' pairts'. When Andrew Melville took over as Principal of Glasgow University in 1574 he established a curriculum which was soon copied by the other Universities. Among the subjects taught were the philosophies of the Renaissance; physics; mathematics; geography; history; Greek; Hebrew; Aramaic; Latin literature and Calvinist theology.

The fact that it took so long to establish a school in every parish was not the fault of Calvin or Calvinism. But Calvinism did encourage education and helped to create the love of learning which rapidly spread throughout the land. By the 18th century Scotland probably had more schools per head of the population than any other country in Europe and obviously had an increasingly literate population.

This resulted in a great increase in the establishment of publishing houses and a rapid development of lending libraries. Books were not printed solely for a social élite as the large number of books circulating shows. Again the evidence points to a wide range of subjects, not all purely of narrow theological interest. The most obvious example is probably Robert Burns. Part of his genius lies in the fact that he had no privileged education, was merely the son of a farmer and only a 'ploughman poet.' Yet even a casual reading of his poems and letters show how widely and deeply he had read. The references to Shakespeare, Pope, Gray, the earlier Scots poets and the classics reveal that he was familiar with the best of literature. Whatever Burns' opinion of Calvin may have been, he was a product of a Calvinist concept of learning – that all men should be able to read and write and have a knowledge, not only of salvation, but the truth that has been revealed even by pagan writers.

John Calvin was certainly not anti-intellectual and his influence upon education in Scotland – its range as well as depth – has been something positive and to the good of the nation. What then did Calvinism give to the arts? Did Calvinism contribute anything to the Scottish Enlightenment?

The Scottish Enlightenment and Calvinism

The growth of literacy, and the demand for literature, undoubtedly helped to open the way for the period known as the 'Scottish Enlightenemnt'. In the 18th century Voltaire could comment that 'at the present time it is from Scotland we receive the rules of taste in all the arts from the Epic Poem to gardening'. While Voltaire is more renowned for his satire and wit than his criticism of the arts, it is a fact that in Scotland there was a great artistic and intellectual flourishing, particularly in the second half of the 18th century.

Common mythology makes Robert Burns the dominant, if not the sole figure, but in reality he was only one among many. In poetry, apart from Burns, there was Robert Fergusson, who greatly influenced the Ayrshire Bard; Allan Ramsay and James Hogg, the Ettrick Shepherd. Ramsay started the first circulating library in Edinburgh in 1725 and later founded a Theatre in Carrubbers Close. In painting there was the younger Ramsay, Nasmyth and Raeburn and the Adam brothers gained deservedly international fame as architects.

Andrew and Robert Foulis founded in Glasgow the famous Foulis Press creating the finest printings of the classics ever seen, printing such works as Homer, Aristotle, Horace and Cicero. They even founded an 'Academy of the Arts' in Glasgow in 1753. The following year the younger Ramsay started 'The Select Society for encouraging Art, Science and Industry' which attracted a large number of eminent Scots including Lord Kames, John Home, the Adam brothers, Adam Smith and even James Boswell. David Hume, although his first book of philosophy in Scotland 'fell stillborn from the Press', was influential in Europe. Indeed the questions his scepticism raised greatly disturbed Emmanuel Kant who confessed that it was Hume who 'awakened him from his slumbers'.

Had Calvinism anything to do with the great flourishing of the arts and sciences in 18th-century Scotland? At first sight it is obvious that the answer must be 'none.' In their lives and works the thinkers and artists of the Scottish Enlightenment were not Calvinists. Indeed the dominant philosophy, and theology, was the product of the 'moderates' — those who placed as much authority, if not more, upon human reasoning than divine revelation.

It seems to me, however, that it is difficult to argue that Calvinism had absolutely nothing to do with the Scottish Enlightenment. The Calvinist emphasis upon broad education must have had the effect of paving the way for an intellectual exploration of all things. It did create a literate population able to read and intelligently discuss the many new ideas that were being engendered.

An even more crucial fact is that, although the Scottish Enlightenment was not Calvinist in philosophy, it did spring from a Calvinist culture. Like all great intellectual and artistic movements, the Scottish Enlightenment did not rise up from nothing; it must have owed something from the past. Flowers must come from seeds and aesthetic flourishing must have some roots. It seems to me that it could be validly argued that the seeds and roots of the Scottish Enlightenment are to be found in Calvinism. Calvin's doctrine of creation and the cultural mandate — man the steward of creation, called to explore and open up all the riches of all the facets of creation — paved the way and gave the energy necessary to pursue knowledge, learning and understanding.

Equally, I suspect, it can be validly argued that the Scottish Enlightenment lost its way, and ran out of energy, because it refused to accept some of the basic tenets of Scripture and Calvinism. It is not human reason but the fear of God that is the beginning of wisdom, and all things, including the arts and sciences, must be subject to the Word of God.

Scottish Genius

In spite of the commonly accepted myth that Calvinist Scotland has been a frustrated land of no artistic opportunity it is a fact that Scotland has produced a remarkable number of eminent men and women. Havelock Ellis, in his work *A Study of British Genius* lists 1030 British men and women who can be rated as having genius. Excluding those of mixed parentage he finds 659 English; 137 Scots; 63 Irish and 28 Welsh and notes the remarkable high proportion of Scots — 15.4% of the total. In a comment on the high number of Scots he remarks that 'intellectual aptitudes are especially marked among the Scots'. Interestingly he notes that it is not purely among the sciences that Scotland excels, but also in the arts with the only exception of drama and acting.

So the question must be asked whether, compared to other nations of a comparable size, Scotland really is a land with a barren artistic history. The arts have had a place in Scotland and, particularly in poetry and literature, the Scots have contributed to the world's rich heritage of art.

Folk song, music and poetry have always had a place in Scotland; even during the upheaval of the Reformation the MacCrimmon school of piping flourished and down through the years the chanter and fiddle have preserved the old music and ballads. Folk singing still has a large following, finding its origins in a simple lifestyle of the past. As the poetry of Burns shows, he had a rich heritage to draw on and, enriching it with his own gifts, he passed it on — perhaps all that any poet can do. The tradition of story-telling has meant that Scotland has produced novelists. Even in the visual arts — painting and architecture particularly — Scotland need not be ashamed.

Calvin has had an influence upon Scotland, his system emphasising reason and logic above emotion and intuition. These need not lead to the death of the arts, but must have a place. If, as many are now suggesting, the arts are really an expression of experience, a celebration transcending reason and, physical reality, then there can be no discussion or debate on the arts. How can we logically talk about something that transcends logic, or reason about something that is beyond reason? It would mean the arts would have to be accepted silently. True art must be the creation of hand, heart and mind.

A great amount of work and study is still required to be done to map out in depth the influence of Calvin in Scotland's artistic heritage. Undoubtedly the history of Scotland has been dominated by theology; indeed the Shorter Catechism seems almost designed to make every child a theologian in embryo. But Calvin's theology was not anti-life, anti-art or anti-joy. It was an attempt to work out a biblical system that would cover all of human life in its theological, social, political and aesthetic facets. He did not work out a 'theology of the arts' but, more importantly, sought to formulate a biblical theology that had a place for the arts and crafts of mankind.

Contrary to the general mythology, the great theme of Calvin was not 'Predestination' but the 'Glory of God.' The heavens declare the glory of God and the earth shows something of His handiwork; men too can show forth that glory in their gifts and abilities. The arts of men are the gift of God, given to glorify God and for the good of men and women.

Perhaps at times in Scotland's history this vision of beauty, joy and creativity being used to glorify and praise God has been lost. If Scotland has been an aesthetically barren desert, a joyless nation, then the blame cannot rest on John Calvin. As we have seen, rather than being the bitter foe of the arts, he accepted what was true, honourable, just, pure, lovely, gracious, excellent and worthy of praise — from whatever source it came — Christian or pagan. He did not deify the arts, making them the highest human activity, but he did show that they have a place in creation, to be used, appreciated and enjoyed.

References

Chapter One
1. Leonardo da Vinci, quoted in *Great Europeans*, ed. John Canning, (Souvenir Press, 1973), p 105.
2. C. S. Lewis, *Screwtape Proposes a Toast and other Essays* (Fontana 1965) pp 118–119.
3. John Calvin, *Commentary on Genesis* (Banner of Truth, 1965), p 217.

Chapter Two
1. John Calvin, *Institutes*, 1/11/12.
2. H. R. Rookmaaker, *Modern Art and the Death of a Culture*, (Inter-Varsity Press, 1970) p 230.
3. Aristotle, from *Classical Literary Criticism* (Penguin Books, 1972) p 44.
4. William Shakespeare, *Hamlet*, Act 2, Scene 2.
5. Abraham Kuyper, quoted in *A Christian Critique of Art and Literature* by Calvin Seerveld (Wedge Publishing Foundation, Canada, 1968) p 29.
6. Pablo Picasso, quoted in *A Theological Approach to Art* by Roger Hazelton (Abingdon Press, USA, 1969) p 16.

Chapter Three
1. Plato, *The Republic* (Penguin Books, 1973) p 384.
2. John Calvin, *Institutes*, 2/2/14.
3. Bertrand Russell, *Mysticism and Logic* (Unwin Books, 1970) p 49.

Chapter Four
1. Jacques Ellul, *The Technological Society* (Vintage Books, USA, 1964) pp 4–5.
2. Gulistan of Moslih Eddin Saadi, in *Best Loved Poems of the American People* (Doubleday, USA. 1936).
3. Eugene Ionesco, Essay 'Facing the Inferno' in *Encounter* Magazine, Nov. 1972.
4. Erich Fromm, *The Dogma of Christ* (Routledge and Kegan Paul, 1963) p 74.
5. William Shakespeare, *Hamlet*, Act 2, Scene 3.
6. William Barrett, *Irrational Man* (Doubleday, USA, 1962) pp 64–65.

7. Franz Kafka, *The Words of Existentialism*, ed. M. Friedman (University of Chicago Press, USA, 1973) p 302.
8. William Shakespeare, *Hamlet*, Act 2, Scene 1.

Chapter Five
1. Martin Esslin, *Absurd Drama* (Penguin Plays, 1969) pp 12–13.
2. Jacques Ellul, op. cit., p 404.
3. Andy Warhol, quoted in *Dictionary of Twentieth Century Art* (Phaidon Press, 1973) p 404.
4. *Official Guide to the Tate Gallery* (1970) p 36.
5. Francis Bacon, quoted in *Dictionary of Twentieth Century Art* (Phaidon Press, 1973) p 19.
6. T. S. Eliot, *Complete Poems and Plays* (Faber and Faber, 1970) p 147.

Chapter Six
1. Peregrin Worsthorne, Essay in *Pornography: the Longford Report* (Coronet Books, 1972) p 131.
2. J. W. Lambert, *The Sunday Times*, 14th April 1974.
3. Andre Breton, quoted in *The History of Surrealism* by M. Nadeau (Penguin Books, 1978) p 22.
4. Albert Camus, ibid, p 23.
5. Eugene Ionesco, op. cit.
6. Eugene Ionesco, ibid.

Chapter Seven
1. Oscar Wilde, *Plays, Prose and Poems* (Everyman Series, J. M. Dent and Sons Ltd., 1950) p 69.
2. Herbert Read, *The Meaning of Art* (Faber and Faber, 1974) p 171.
3. Calvin Seerveld, *A Christian Critique of Art and Literature* (Wedge Publishing Foundation, Canada, 1968) p 28.
4. H. R. Rookmaaker, Essay on 'Christian Art' in *Encyclopedia of Christianity* (National Foundation for Christian Education, USA, 1968).
5. John Calvin, quoted in *Lectures on Calvinism* by Abraham Kuyper (Associated Publishers and Authors, USA undated) p 97.
6. Harry Blamires, *The Christian Mind* (S.P.C.K., 1963) p 10.

Chapter Eight
1. John Milton, 'Paradise Lost' from *Poetic Works* (F. Warne and Co., undated) p 282.
2. Albert Camus, *The Myth of Sisyphus* (Penguin Books, 1975) pp 191–192.
3. John Calvin, *Commentary on Genesis* (Banner of Truth, 1965) p 217.

4. Martin Luther, quoted in *Here I Stand* by Roland H Bainton (Mentor Books, USA, 1963) p 269.

Chapter Nine
1. Oscar Wilde, op. cit. p 70.
2. John Calvin, *Institutes*, 2/2/15.
3. Abraham Kuyper, quoted in *Literature and the Gospel* by M. Meeter (Presbyterian and Reformed Publishers, USA, 1972) p 13.
4. John Calvin, *Institutes*, 2/2/14.
5. Bernard Zylstra, *Will All the King's Men?* (Wedge Publishing Foundation, Canada, 1972) p 157.
6. John Calvin, *Institutes*, 2/2/15.
7. Pablo Picasso, *Picasso Says*, ed. Helene Parmelin (Allen and Unwin, 1969) p 70.
8. John Calvin, quoted in *Lectures on Calvinism* by Abraham Kuyper (Associated Publishers and Authors, USA, undated) p 97.

Chapter Ten
1. Pope Gregory, quoted in Essay on 'Christian Art' in *The Catholic Encyclopedia* (USA 1908).
2. Abraham Kuyper, *Lectures on Calvinism* (Associated Publishers and Authors, USA, undated) p 87.
3. John Calvin, *Institutes*, 1/11/12.
4. John Calvin, quoted in *The Calvinist Concept of Culture* by H. R. van Til Presbyterian and Reformed Publishers, USA, 1972) p 110.
5. John Calvin, ibid, p 110.
6. *The Westminister Confession of Faith*, chapter 21, para 1.
7. John Calvin, *Golden Booklet of the True Christian Life* (Evangelical Press, 1975) p 88.
8. John Davison, Essay 'Reformation in the Meeting House' in *Reformation Today* magazine, Sept/Oct 1975.

Chapter Eleven
1. H. R. Rookmaaker, *Modern Art and the Death of a Culture* (Inter-Varsity Press, 1970) p 228.
2. T. S. Eliot, quoted in *Sourcebook of Poetry*, ed. Al Bryant (Zonderman, USA, 1968) p 6.
3. E. J. Mishan, Essay 'To Grow or not to Grow' in *Encounter* Magazine, May 1973.
4. Martin Luther, quoted in *Here I Stand* by Roland H Bainton (Mentor Books, USA, 1963) pp 236–237.

5. William Morris, *Industrialisation and Culture*, ed. Harvie, Martin and Scharf (Open University Press, 1970) p 195.
6. Calvin Seerveld, op. cit., p 29.

Chapter Twelve
1. Maurice Wilkins, quoted in *Oh, What a Blow that Phantom Gave Me!* by Edmund Carpenter (Paladin Books, 1976) p 55.
2. H. R. Rookmaaker, op. cit., p 220.
3. Eugene Ionesco, op. cit.
4. H. R. Rookmaaker, op. cit., p 245.
5. George Orwell, *Tribune* magazine, 3rd March 1944.
6. John Calvin, quoted in *Calvin and the Sciences* by Nigel Nee (Sovereign Grace Union, 1969) p 44.
7. Calvin Seerveld, op. cit., pp 28–29.
8. John Calvin, quoted in *Calvin and the Sciences* by Nigel Nee (Sovereign Grace Union, 1969) p 44.
9. Abraham Kuyper, op. cit., p 99.

Bibliography

There are innumerable books on the arts and many have been quoted in the text of this study. The following is a list of some books which I have not actually quoted but have found to be useful and stimulating. Not all are written by Christians but they all have something to add to our understanding of 'one of the richest gifts of God to mankind'.

S. B. Babbage, *The Mark of Cain*, Paternoster Press, 1966.

H. Blamires, *A Short History of English Literature*, Methuen & Co., 1974.

R. G. Collingwood, *The Principles of Art*, Oxford University Press, 1974.

W. A. Dyrness, *Rouault: A Vision of Suffering and Salvation*, Eerdmans, (USA) 1972.

Havelock Ellis, *A Study of British Genius*, Constable & Co., 1927.

Ruth Etchells, *Unafraid to Be*, Inter-Varsity Press, 1969.

G. S. Fraser, *The Modern Writer and His World*, Penguin, 1970.

B. Gasgoigne, *Twentieth Century Drama*, Hutchison, 1974.

E. H. Gombrich, *The Story of Art*, Phaidon Press, 1966.

B. Griffiths, *Art, Pornography and Human Value*, Grove Booklets, 1975.

D. Holbrook, *The Pseudo-Revolution*, Tom Stacey, 1972.

O. R. Johnston, *Christianity in a Collapsing Culture*, Paternoster Press, 1976.

H. Read, *A Concise History of Modern Painting*, Thames and Hudson, 1975.

H. R. Rookmaaker, *Art and the Public Today*, L'Abri Fellowship Foundation, 1969.

H. R. Rookmaaker, *Gauguin and 19th Century Art Theory*, Swets and Zeitlinger, Amsterdam, 1972.

F. A. Schaeffer, *The God Who is There*, Hodder and Stoughton, 1974.

F. A. Schaeffer, *Art and the Bible*, Hodder and Stoughton, 1974.

E. B. Tennyson & E. Ericson (eds), *Religion and Modern Literature*, Eerdmans, USA 1975.